PRAISE FOR OTHER ~~~~
BY AHMED OSMAN

The Hebrew Pharaohs of Egypt
"In *The Hebrew Pharaohs of Egypt*, Ahmed Osman singlehand-
edly moves the goalposts of biblical scholarship. He successfully
narrows the search for the historical Hebrew patriarchs by giving
us a novel and persuasive case for a secret lineage of the patriarch
Joseph. This is a must read for all alternative history buffs and
scholars alike."

RAND FLEM-ATH, COAUTHOR OF *ATLANTIS BENEATH THE ICE*
AND *THE ATLANTIS BLUEPRINT*

Breaking the Mirror of Heaven
"This is a book that needed to be written . . . and I can't imagine a better writing team to have taken on the challenge. Robert
Bauval and Ahmed Osman have expertly untangled the history of
the Egyptian Antiquities Organization, in all its guises, and successfully exposed the trauma of the Zahi Hawass years. This is a
story that should be read by all those interested in Egyptology and
everyone who cares passionately about Egypt . . . a tour de force in
modern historical investigation."

DAVID ROHL, EGYPTOLOGIST, HISTORIAN,
BROADCASTER, AND AUTHOR OF *A TEST OF TIME*

"Egyptology has lied to us for too long. Now a meticulous investigation by two top authors reveals the disturbing truth. This book
is dynamite."

GRAHAM HANCOCK,
AUTHOR OF *FINGERPRINTS OF THE GODS*

"Bauval and Osman's *Breaking the Mirror of Heaven* ('Mirror of Heaven' is the name given to Egypt by Hermes-Thoth) is not just about Hawass and his monumental ego and failings; it is an attempt to reveal the truth about the desecration of artifacts over the centuries, the effects of foreign rule, the suppression of 'pagan' wisdom, the Freemasonry-inspired Napoleonic invasion, and the political power plays in the post-war era from Nasser to Mubarak that continue morphing to this day."

NEXUS MAGAZINE

"Prolific writers with in-depth knowledge of ancient Egypt, Robert Bauval and Ahmed Osman have teamed up to produce a scathing indictment of former Egyptian Minister of Antiquities Zahi Hawass."

NEW DAWN MAGAZINE

Moses and Akhenaten
"The classic work that redefines the timeframe of the Exodus and places it firmly in the age of Akhenaten and Tutankhamun. Essential reading for all Bible historians."

ANDREW COLLINS, AUTHOR OF *GOBEKLI TEPE*, *FROM THE ASHES OF ANGELS*, AND *GATEWAY TO ATLANTIS*

THE
LOST CITY
OF THE
EXODUS

The Archaeological Evidence
behind the Journey Out of Egypt

AHMED OSMAN

Bear & Company
Rochester, Vermont • Toronto, Canada

Bear & Company
One Park Street
Rochester, Vermont 05767
www.BearandCompanyBooks.com

Text stock is SFI certified

Bear & Company is a division of Inner Traditions International

Library of Congress Cataloging-in-Publication Data

Osman, Ahmed.
  The lost city of the exodus : the archaeological evidence behind the journey out
of egypt / Ahmed Osman.
      p. cm.
    Includes bibliographical references and index.
    ISBN 978-1-59143-189-3 (pbk.) — ISBN 978-1-59143-771-0 (e-book)
    1. Egypt—Antiquities. 2. Excavations (Archaeology)—Egypt. 3. Exodus, The. 4.
Yuya. 5. Akhenaton, King of Egypt. 6. Moses (Biblical leader) I. Title.
    DT60.O85 2014
    932'.014—dc23

                                                                    2013036461

Printed and bound in the United States by Lake Book Manufacturing, Inc.
The text stock is SFI certified. The Sustainable Forestry Initiative® program
promotes sustainable forest management.

10 9 8 7 6 5 4 3 2 1

Text design and layout by Brian Boynton
This book was typeset in Garamond Premier Pro with Trebuchet, Gill Sans, and
Papyrus used as display typefaces

To send correspondence to the author of this book, mail a first-class letter to the
author c/o Inner Traditions • Bear & Company, One Park Street, Rochester, VT
05767, and we will forward the communication, or contact the author directly at
aosman2017@gmail.com.

To the memory of
Sigmund Freud
a brave and honest man with a vision

CONTENTS

PROLOGUE

I was asked an intriguing question by George Hill of the *London Times,* in October 1987. As he was getting ready to write a comment on my first book regarding the identification of Yuya, a minister of Amenhotep III, and patriarch Joseph of the coat of many colors, he asked me: "How could you arrive to this important identification, when many other senior scholars, could not?" "They couldn't because it didn't agree with their beliefs," I answered. He then asked me: "And what do you believe in?" to which I said: "I believe in what I find."

It was true, although it took a long time to come to this objective position, with no taboos and no obsessions. However, during my years of research I came across many scholars who were ready to reject the objective conclusions, just because those conclusions didn't agree with their beliefs. Before publishing my book about Joseph, I contacted Cyril Aldred, the Scottish Egyptologist, in Edinburgh. As he had stated in his book about Akhenaten that Yuya's mummy shows him to be a foreigner of Semitic origin, I asked him if I could identify him as Joseph. Not only did Aldred reject this identification, he also removed his comment on Yuya's Semitic origin from the next edition of his book.

Later, following the publication of my book, I was contacted by someone from the NBC TV station in the United States who was doing a program called *Lost and Found.* He wanted me to appoint someone in America who could defend my argument on his program. As I had met him at the International Congress of Egyptologists, and he had agreed that the time of Yuya is the right time for Joseph, I asked the

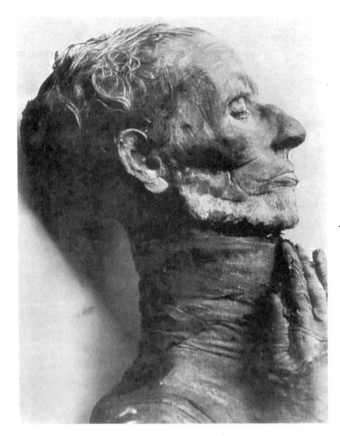

Fig. P.1. The mummy of Yuya, from my book The Hebrew Pharaohs of Egypt.

American Egyptologist James K. Hoffmeier to represent me. To my surprise, Hoffmeier refused. I asked why not, as long as he does agree with me. He said: "It is against my religion."

Again, although I was trying, as was he, to find historical evidence to confirm the biblical account of the Israelite Exodus from Egypt, Kenneth Kitchen of Liverpool University could not agree on a single point of my research. For while I, being an Egyptian, was trying to uncover the historical reality of Moses and the Exodus, Kitchen, as a Christian, wanted to verify the historicity of the biblical narrative in its literal sense. He once told me: If an Egyptian text disagrees with a biblical text, I would accept the authority of the Bible.

Later, when I asked Farouk Hosni, Egypt's Minister of Culture, who was also responsible for its antiquities, to allow a DNA test on Yuya's mummy to make sure of his origin, he refused. I told him if

Fig. P.2. Professor Kenneth Kitchen with Ahmed Osman.
Photo courtesy of Ahmed Osman.

Yuya's genes prove to be similar to Upper Egyptians, I would accept that the identification with Joseph is wrong, but, on the other hand, if his genes proved to be similar to those living in Palestine, Hosni should accept that I have a point. The minister refused. He said that even if Yuya's genes proved to be non-Egyptian, he could not accept my conclusion, as this would create a political problem with the Israeli government, who could demand Joseph's mummy. I explained that, according to international agreements, objects of antiquity belong to the country where they are found. At the same time, the Israeli government would not dare to demand Joseph's mummy, as it would contradict the biblical statement that Moses had taken the body of Joseph with him at the time of the Exodus. Nevertheless, Hosni could not agree.

One autumn afternoon, I met Zahi Hawass on the grounds of the Castello Valentino in the Italian city of Turin. It was September 8, 1991, the closing day of the Sixth International Congress of Egyptology, and all those who had attended this prestigious event had been invited to a farewell party in the Castello Valentino gardens. I was sitting in the garden with some members of the Egyptian delegation, including Dr. Ali Hassan, who was Director of Antiquities, and Zahi Hawass, who was, at the time, Director of the Giza Plateau.

Four years earlier, I had written a book titled *Stranger in the Valley of the Kings: The Identification of Yuya as the Patriarch Joseph* in which I had argued that the famous biblical character was probably the same person as Yuya, an important courtier of the Eighteenth Dynasty whose mummy was displayed in the Cairo Museum, and who had been grand vizier (a minister) to pharaoh Thutmose IV. Yuya eventually became Akhenaten's grandfather (his daughter, Queen Tiye, was Akhenaten's mother); and because I had declared Yuya's mummy to have clearly Semitic features, Hawass had dismissed my research as part of a Zionist cultural plot to give Egyptian pharaohs a Hebrew ancestry.

Then, exactly a year before the Congress, my second book had come out. It was called *Moses: Pharaoh of Egypt* and this time I had progressed beyond the identification of Joseph with Akhenaten's grandfather: I had actually shown that Akhenaten and Moses were one and the same person. This new book, naturally, had been the subject of our conversation and in no time at all Hawass had pulled up a chair and begun to trash my thesis. Not on its merits, of course, but on its supposed motivations.

"I'm telling you, Osman, yours is not history, it's just Jewish propaganda!"

"It's only a hypothesis," I interjected. "If a team of scientists were to examine the DNA of Yuya's mummy and confirm that he came, not from Canaan, but from Upper Egypt, I would be ready to abandon my argument."

Hawass's chest rose visibly. "And who are you to even suggest that such an examination should be carried out?" Then he looked at me, his eyes narrowing threateningly.

"Who are you, Osman? You're just an amateur. You're not an antiquities man, you're not even an archaeologist! Let me tell you something," and here his tone rose to those of apocalyptic prophecy. "Even if it were possible, *we*, the scientists, will never examine the DNA of Yuya's mummy. Never!"

The level of his voice had drawn three or four other delegates to the vicinity of our part of the garden, while the Egyptians I had been conversing with were visibly embarrassed by Hawass's outburst. But Hawass was not through with me: "As for your latest fantasy on Akhenaten, you should know that they offered me *a million dollars* to write a book about Akhenaten, how can one of our pharaohs have a mixed Jewish blood?" "What is wrong with Jewish blood?" I asked, "Our prophet Muhammad was a descendant of Abraham, the great ancestor of the Israelites."

I finished my glass of wine and placed it calmly on the table. Then I spoke firmly, but quite softly. "Do you know what the difference is between you and me?" I asked him.

Fig. P.3. Akhenaten at the Cairo Museum. Photo courtesy of Ahmed Osman.

Hawass didn't answer, waiting to hear my words, a sneer already on his face.

"The difference between you and me is that despite not having a job with the antiquities, I am constantly contacted by the press for my views on historical questions, because I have something to say. As for you, they only need you for the permits you issue, and the day after you leave your official position, no one will even remember your name."

Hawass glowered for a few moments, perhaps weighing the possibility of slugging me. Then he stood up, mumbling something under his breath, and walked away with long, angry steps.

Can such a prejudiced attitude help scholars to reach the right conclusion?

INTRODUCTION

THE BROTHERHOOD, COMMUNISM, AND MOSES

I was born in Cairo in 1934 and lost my father while still a boy of eight years old. In many senses, Egyptian society was more progressive and open-minded in the thirties than it is now, but the trauma of losing one's paternal guidance at such a vulnerable age prevented me from entering society in a balanced, responsible way. I needed the spiritual support of a great father, so I started to look for God.

Soon I was getting up at dawn, praying and reading the Qur'an until it was time to go to school. And it was the religious teacher at my primary school who became the first strong influence on my adolescent thoughts. He was a charismatic man with a stocky build, a fez on his head, a well-trimmed beard and fiery eyes. When he laid his thick hands on my desk, I used to look up at his half-open mouth, which gave me the impression that he was always smiling.

His name was Hassan al-Banna.*

Yes, the founder of the Muslim Brotherhood was my first teacher, and in hindsight I can see how I came to be a moralistic firebrand before I had even experienced what temptation—i.e., free thinking and

---

*Hassan al-Banna is best known for founding the Muslim Brotherhood, one of the largest and most influential Muslim organizations, which, in the 1930s, had 500,000 active members.

1

girls—was all about. During lunch break I would run to the school mosque for midday prayers where I would meet young members of the Brotherhood. We would sit in a circle as their leader read us the story of one of the "Prophet's Companions," or some other hero of early Islam, explaining how they were able to defeat the enemies of God. Naturally, they invited me to join their circle and soon managed to persuade me to join the Brotherhood. Following God's path, they said, is what will allow us to build a strong nation and defeat the enemies of Allah, who at that time were clearly and forcefully identified for me as the government, the British colonial forces, and the Jews in Palestine: in that order.

In 1947, when the United Nations announced the partition of Palestine into an Arab and a Jewish state, the Muslim Brothers began calling for volunteers to go and fight the Jews in Palestine, to prevent the establishment of a state of Israel. I was told that if I joined the fight against the Jews I could expect one of two results: either I would be victorious and help defeat the enemies of God, or I would die as a martyr and go straight to paradise. To me, this sounded like the best deal I could possibly get, a free ticket to paradise. To my chagrin, when I applied to join the volunteers I was refused on account of my age. It was 1948 and I was only fourteen: two years below the minimum age to join the jihad.

As I related above, in 1948 the Brotherhood, whose volunteer squads had fought well against Israel, entered into conflict with the government. Within less than a year from Ben-Gurion's declaration of independence, both the Egyptian Prime Minister and Hassan al-Banna had been murdered. Thousands of Muslim Brothers were either in jail or had escaped into exile, and our little group had to meet in secret. Older brothers were undergoing military training somewhere in the desert, but the Ikhwan's* instructions for those of us who were underage were to hide our relation with the Society as best we could, and to behave like ordinary boys.

I was fifteen and, Muslim Brother or not, testosterone was accu-

*Brotherhood

Fig. I.1. Hassan al-Banna. Courtesy of the Muslim Brotherhood website.

mulating in my bloodstream like in that of any healthy boy of that age. Before the crackdown, I would spend my free time rushing to meetings with the Brothers, looking at the ground in front of me as I walked to avoid committing a sin by seeing a part—almost any part—of a girl's body. Now I had been explicitly instructed to behave like ordinary boys. Before the crackdown, as I got ready for bed at night, I would go through the long list I had been given and count the sins I had committed during the day: did I tell a lie, did I miss a prayer, did I look at a girl's body; in short, did I commit any action that transgressed the Shari'a, or Islamic Law? Now, not only did I no longer have to monitor myself on behalf of my mentors, I was actually supposed to commit some of those sins in order to look like an ordinary boy.

This opened new doors for me. I started to go to the movies, I listened to love songs for the first time, I missed more and more of my prayers and, perhaps most importantly as I think back on those days, I started to look at girls. The effort to repress my teenage instincts gone, I began to watch every beautiful girl in the street.

Somewhat to my surprise, I liked it.

Another major taboo at the Brotherhood—possibly more dangerous, in the long run, than girls—had been philosophy. Now I found that not only was philosophy among the subjects taught in the class I had just reached at school, but that if I didn't want to raise the teachers' suspicions, I would have to read those dangerous books. Philosophy classes were strange and surprising. Here, the teacher didn't go on about God the creator punishing all sinners, and there was no talk of hell or paradise, just the cosmos and the mind, occasionally called "spirit." Some of the philosophers whose writings were discussed denied God's very existence, while others accepted him, though they resorted to calling him the "Great Mind" or "Spirit."

The Brotherhood would have called all these thinkers "unbelievers" and severely punished anyone caught reading them, but I was sixteen and starting to exhibit the traits that would define my intellectual career: a stubborn determination to figure things out for myself, to think with my own head instead of accepting "received" knowledge. I wanted to know more, so I started to go to the public library—on the quiet—and consult books about Socrates, Plato, and Aristotle. The more I read, the more life's mysteries seemed to be much deeper than I had thought. Within a year of al-Banna's assassination God had been taken away from me, and I felt twice orphaned, a confused mind distracted by a rapidly changing world—and girls—from its efforts to find the meaning of life.

It was 1950 and Egyptian "coffeehouse society" was thriving. The atmosphere in Cairo and Alexandria was still—as in the mythical 1930s—a blend of intellectual curiosity and sensual joie-de-vivre. One can still catch a whiff of it spiralling up from the pages of *Naguib Mahfouz* or Lawrence Durrell's *Alexandrian Quartet* like lazy smoke rings from a hookah. That was the atmosphere in which I first met some members of the underground Egyptian Communist Party.

Frequent conversations with several revolutionary youngsters and one or two grown-up Marxist intellectuals disabused me of the last traces of the religious extremism that had dominated half of my short, gullible life. Karl Marx and Friedrich Engels, I was told, had made it clear for everyone that nothing exists in the universe beyond the physical world. What we call God is nothing but a construct of the human mind, which dies when we die. What men need, it was pretty obvious once your eyes were opened, is not a just God, but a just government. History was but the account of the struggle between two classes, rich and poor, owners and workers. If we could only overthrow the pres-

Fig. I.2. Karl Marx. Courtesy of the Guardian, *February 17, 2012.*

ent government and replace it with a communist one, like in the Soviet Union, people would be happy; with each man doing what he can and getting what he needs (this was Arab communism, and women did not figure in it).

Contrary to the Brothers, with the communists there was no need to die a martyr's death to gain entrance to paradise; they promised paradise on Earth. To their credit, in that period the Egyptian Communist Party also opposed the war against the newly established state of Israel and had good relations with Jewish comrades, especially the ones in Paris, Rome, and Moscow.

The first pamphlet I was given by the comrades, *The Truth* (i.e. *Pravda*), had a red hammer and sickle printed on its cover, and I had to hide in our bathroom to read it. I was now one of the people "on the right side of history," the ones who were going to change the world and bring justice to the oppressed by establishing a dictatorship of the working class. This made me feel really important. I started ignoring my homework, busy as I was studying political and economic pamphlets and attending secret meetings with the comrades. Besides trying to recruit new members, our political activity was focused on organizing student strikes and marches, in which we loudly called for the overthrow of the government and the downfall of King Farouk.

As I recounted earlier, 1951 saw the growth of tensions with the British, culminating in the abrogation of the Anglo-Egyptian Treaty in October. The Brothers, despite being harshly repressed since murdering the prime minister three years earlier, were engaged in a campaign of what would now be called "terrorism." Students and activists, whether communist or religious, were united in an antigovernment, anticolonial frenzy. Then, in January 1952, the massacre of policemen at Isma'iliyya took place. Early the next day, a secret message from the comrades was delivered to us at school, instructing us to organize marches and meet at Cairo University for a massive demonstration. I was among the leaders at our school, herding students into the street while shouting slogans with that heady mix of fear and excitement that every twentieth-century student has known and loved.

At one point, as we approached Opera Square in central Cairo, I saw some older men getting out of a truck with cans full of gasoline, which they splashed on the well-known Badi'a nightclub, quickly setting fire to it. In a feeling of camaraderie with everyone whose outrage was spilling into the streets, I asked them why they had chosen that particular target, but they were in an obvious hurry to complete a preordained plan and didn't bother to answer me. By the time we reached Isma'iliyya Square (now Tahrir Square), most of central Cairo's shopping district was on fire, looters breaking into stores and carrying away what they could. We never reached the university, and by evening the king had declared martial law. In hindsight, I had clearly been a witness to one of many occasions in which history is given "a little push" by cynical players making carefully manipulated events seem totally spontaneous.

In an attempt to calm the situation, King Farouk dismissed Nahhas Pasha's government, but four prime ministers held office in the following six months, and things were anything but calm. Our hopes of riding popular anger all the way to a communist revolution were dashed during the night of July 22, when Nasser's Free Officers made their move, beating us across the political finish. Their military coup changed the course of Egyptian history.

Sometimes I think it changed the course of my life, too.

By the time I was twenty and enrolled at Ain Shams University in Cairo to study law, I had become responsible for communist party activity in the western Nile Delta. It was 1954, and Nasser's government was rapidly turning into a regime, with the screws being turned on any sort of opposition. Unbeknownst to any of us, the security police had managed to infiltrate the communist party's organization, and one day I was suddenly arrested—together with sixty other party members, including the chairman—for illegal activities against the state.

The truth is that by then my reflections had already begun to undermine my faith in the communist utopia, and I no longer relished the idea of sacrificing my youth to a political ideal in the hope of becoming a cadre who could one day claim to have spent time in jail under the dictator. I was still reading philosophy and had found my way to French existentialists like Jean-Paul Sartre and Albert Camus. The idea sat well with me, by this time, that there wasn't much point in looking for meaning in life, as it has neither meaning nor purpose. I would have to give up all hope of salvation, I thought, but perhaps once I had done that, I could finally get on with my life.

Fig. I.3. Gamal Abdel Nasser. Courtesy of Bibliotheca Alexandrina.

I was lucky enough to be released from prison early, before the court hearing was even held, and went straight back to my law studies; all thoughts of religion and politics forced out of my head. Having obtained my degree, I went to work as a journalist at *Akhbar el Yom,* then the most widely circulated daily newspaper in Egypt. My job was to cover society news and events, which meant meeting and getting to know some of the most prominent members of the Cairo elite, especially artists and intellectuals.

Moving in these circles I was attracted to the theater, which flourished in Egypt at that time, and tried my hand at writing some plays. But though four of my plays were published in books, the censors refused to allow any of them to be produced for the stage. The reason was always one of the same three: politics, religion, or sex. Eventually, in 1964, one play was produced, but when someone suggested that it could be filmed for TV or made into a movie, permission was refused. Except for my occasional troubles with the censors, I liked being a journalist and loved the stimulating social life. But something inside me was starting to cause a profound irritation. It was the ubiquitous rhetoric of war against the Jews.

By the early sixties it was clear that Nasser was getting ready for the final confrontation with Israel. It was in the air. He was buying more and more Russian weapons and at one point even brought military experts from the Soviet Union to train the Egyptian army.

I didn't like it. All Egyptian territory under British or Israeli occupation had been liberated, so this war, like the tripartite invasion of the Sinai in 1956, would be regarded by the world as an attack on a sovereign state, and Egypt would face universal condemnation. What's more, after being denied the chance to fight the Jews in 1948 because I was underage, now that I had done my military service and could be drafted in any future war, I was no longer sure that fighting the Jews was good or justified.

Not that I had become a pacifist, but while as a young Muslim Brother I was willing to kill Jews to gain my way into paradise, now I was no longer sure where right and wrong really lay. It seemed to me that the war could be as holy for the other side as it was for us. Unlike colonial Britain and France, the Israelis clearly had no intention of "going home," as Yankees in Central America were often told to do, because they regarded Palestine as their only home. If Arabs and Jews both had a claim to the land and were, so to speak, partially in the right, I wanted to understand why it was so difficult for us to sit down with the Israelis and *talk*. After all, military conflicts have always ended with political agreements. France and Germany were a perfect example, having become close friends after centuries of wars. I realized that there must be a taboo, something deep and unspoken by either side that didn't allow us to break the barriers and shake hands.

This effort—understanding the real reasons behind the undying enmity between Egypt and Israel—gradually became the intellectual obsession that replaced my earlier yearnings. As I thought about it, I decided to write a play on the Exodus. I discussed the issue with Tawfik el Hakeem, a well-known Egyptian playwright, and he advised me to read the biblical Book of Exodus. Muslims don't usually read the Bible; they get their knowledge of Judaism and Christianity from their own Islamic sources (i.e. the Qur'an and all its commentaries). Still, I bought a copy of the Bible in Arabic and used the Book of Exodus as the principal source for my play, which I called *Where Is Paradise?*

The play's ironic theme was that, had the Israelites stayed in Egypt instead of leaving for Canaan, they would have become Egyptians and avoided all the later, well-known troubles in their history. Paradise, I implied, was a home that we accept and in which we are accepted. The play was published as a book, but I wasn't really satisfied with it. What bothered me was that though the events in the play took place in ancient Egypt, I had made recourse to the Bible rather than ancient Egyptian sources. In my mind sacred scriptures, even when they include accounts of historical characters and events, could not be considered reliable historical sources.

So I decided to start again. I would write another dramatic work on the event that was to become the cornerstone of the Jewish Bible, the Israelite Exodus from Egypt; but this time I would rely on evidence from ancient Egyptian records. Tawfik el Hakeem and two other authors, Yehya Haqqy and Muhammad Mandoor, supported my application for a one-year government grant, during which time I planned to research the Egyptian evidence for Israel in Egypt.

I was absolutely certain that if the Bible story of Moses, which is also found in the Qur'an, represented real historical events, and not just a mythological account written to strengthen the believers' faith, then I should be able to find evidence of it in the history of ancient Egypt. And, more importantly, I was just as convinced that if I could find the truth about Moses and the Exodus, I would be able to understand the roots of the feud between Jews and Egyptians, which had lasted over three millennia, and showed no sign of approaching reconciliation.

First I went to the Cairo Museum to see the myriad of statues and other remains of the pharaonic period, but I found nothing there about Moses or the Exodus. Egyptian libraries weren't much more helpful: there was nothing on the subject. Perhaps only the Cairo Museum Library might have been of use to me, as it housed books and periodicals written by foreign archaeologists who worked in Egypt, but that library—this is an understatement—was not structured to help readers find what they were looking for. Piles of books were stacked in every available corner with almost no references to guide a search.

To be fair, the Cairo Museum Library in the early 1960s was also a truly magical place. Almost every one of the eccentrics I met there would have deserved having a Borges-like novel written about him, had I felt so inclined. More than once I found myself toying with the idea of hiding somewhere and staying in the museum after closing time, to see if there were any *jinns* (malevolent or benevolent spirits) in the place, and to experience the atmosphere in a darkened warehouse storing 4,000 years of memories.

But by the time the government grant expired, it had become clear to me that there was only one place on Earth where I could find everything I needed for my research, and that place was the Library of the British Museum. That's when I decided to leave Cairo and go to London, where I began looking for evidence for biblical Qur'anic stories in Egyptian sources.

Egypt was without doubt a place of great importance in the Bible, in which it is one of the most frequently mentioned places. Its presence spans both the Old and the New Testaments, from Genesis to the Gospels. But of all the Bible stories involving Egypt, it is the Israelites' oppression and exodus from there that eventually became the cornerstone of the book. However, perhaps the most important clue, in hindsight, that lead me to develop my own understanding of the Exodus came not from Bible studies or Egyptology, but from the little-frequented discipline of psychohistory, founded by the father of psychoanalysis, Sigmund Freud.

Freud, the Jewish founder of the psychoanalytical school of psychology, is best known for his theories of the unconscious mind. But in the thirties, perhaps because of the growing persecution of Jews by Hitler in Nazi Germany, he invested much time and thought in the effort to understand the reasons behind modern anti-Semitism. In March 1938, Nazi Germany annexed Austria, and Freud, amid intense outbursts of violence against Viennese Jews, decided to leave his country and go to England with his family.

His research on the origins of the Jewish religion, and in particular on Moses, yielded unusual results: Freud claimed to have found traces of Moses and the Exodus not at the time of Ramses II and the Nineteenth Dynasty, but at the time of Akhenaten and the Eighteenth

Fig. I.4. Sigmund Freud. Photo courtesy of Freud's Museum, London.

Dynasty. Once safely in London, he published his controversial ideas in his last book, *Moses and Monotheism,* just a few months before dying in September 1939, three weeks after Hitler's tanks had rolled across the Polish border.

The study was a human mind's glimpse deep into the hidden past, into the collective unconscious of mankind. Freud, who was trying to understand the reason behind the continuous hatred of the Jews, followed neither the evidence of archaeology nor biblical criticism, but looked deep in the human mind: the unconscious. After all, it is generally agreed that the Torah, the first five books of the Old Testament, were composed and compiled over several hundred years between the tenth and the sixth century BCE. The scribes, relying on human memory, wrote down a much older oral tradition, some of which may have gone back to more than eight centuries earlier.

In his book, Freud argued that the Bible's Moses was actually an ancient Egyptian official, a follower of the monotheistic king Akhenaten, father of Tutankhamun. Much more interestingly in *Moses and Monotheism,* Freud also argued that Moses was murdered by the Israelites in the wilderness. Freud, after concluding that Moses had indeed been killed by his own followers, built further on the idea, introducing a phenomenon he had himself discovered, neurosis, into the analysis of Jewish religious history.

Neurosis, as explained by Freud, is the result of a fantasized battle that takes place in the subconscious of each person, out of reach of waking consciousness. It occurs in a realm of mind that is something like a virtual reality, in which illusory versions of ourselves seek to win over, escape, and overpower an imaginary version of the primary caretakers of childhood. As Freud saw it, the child's only way of dealing with a traumatizing event is its denial. As a result, the trauma enters a latency period where it is sorted—elaborated, processed, metabolized—until it eventually resurfaces as the return of the repressed during puberty, expressing itself as obsessive neurosis or phobia.

Years after the murder, the rebels fashioned a Jewish religion that promoted Moses as the Savior of the Israelites. In other words, following a lengthy period of latency, Moses and his doctrines reemerged and became even more powerful and obsessive. Freud seized on the parallelism with his own etiology of neurosis and deduced that when they adopted Moses's monotheism, the Jews were denying the earlier events surrounding the death of their leader. Just as in neurosis, so Moses's return in monotheism is a compromise struck in which something is remembered, but incorrectly.

Although he was not a theologian or a biblical scholar, but a researcher of human psychology, Freud introduced many new elements into the debate that I had been following since my arrival in London. He was the first one, for example, to make the connection between Moses and Akhenaten, the monotheistic king of Egypt. However, no academic scholar was ready to take Freud's challenge seriously, and most historians rejected the legitimacy of his particular theory of psychohistory. For a start, archaeologists and biblical scholars could not accept it because according to their chronology, Moses could not be found in the Eighteenth Dynasty.

1

THE STORY OF THE EXODUS

The biblical account of the Israelites' Exodus from Egypt is one of the most popular narratives from the ancient world. It is the theme of the Jewish festival of Passover, "Pesach," which refers to God's instruction to the Israelites to mark their doors with the blood of slaughtered lamb so that the Lord would "pass over" them on his way to kill Egypt's first-born. It is also celebrated by the Christians who regard it as the feast of Maundy Thursday, the night on which the Last Supper is generally thought to have taken place.

Nobody who reads the Bible can fail to notice that the main purpose of the Pentateuch (or Torah), the first five books of the Old Testament, is to tell the story of the relationship between Egypt and Israel. Following the creation and the flood accounts, the rest of the Pentateuch has only one main subject to report, the relation between the Hebrew tribe of Israel and the royal family of Egypt. Abraham, the grandfather of Israel, was the first to make contact with the Pharaohs, when he went down from Canaan to Egypt with his wife Sarah. As he didn't want the Egyptians to know that Sarah was his wife, Abraham told her: "Please say that you are my sister so that it may go well with me because of you, and that I may live on account of you" (Genesis 12:13). Soon after their arrival to the country, Abram (Abraham) and Sarah were able to establish contact directly with the pharaonic royal family:

> It came about when Abram came into Egypt, the Egyptians saw that the woman was very beautiful. Pharaoh's officials saw her and praised her to Pharaoh; and the woman (Sarah) was taken into Pharaoh's house. Therefore he treated Abram well for her sake; and gave him sheep and oxen and he donkeys and male and female servants and female donkeys and camels. (Genesis 12:14–16)

However, this relation between Pharaoh and Sarah, Abraham's wife, caused the Egyptian king much trouble. The Lord "inflicted serious diseases" on him and his household, and, once he realized the cause of his problems, Pharaoh summoned Abraham and asked: "What is this that you have done to me? Why did you not tell me that she was your wife? Why did you say, 'She is my sister,' so that *I took her for my wife*? Now then, here is your wife, take her and go" (Genesis 12:18–19). Then Abraham took Sarah his wife and all his possessions and returned to Canaan. But before she left, Pharaoh gave Sarah an Egyptian maid named Hagar.

Thus Abraham and Sarah, the parents of Isaac and the grandparents of Jacob who later became known as Israel, were the first of the Hebrews to go down to Egypt and establish a close relation with the Egyptian royal family. Although Pharaoh sent them back to Canaan, the life of Abraham and Sarah changed completely as a result of their Egyptian visit, and Egypt haunted them for the rest of their lives. Following their return to Canaan the Lord told Abraham, in a vision, that his wife Sarah will bear him a son whom he will call Isaac, and with whom the Lord shall establish his everlasting covenant. The Lord also told him that his descendants from Sarah will go back to Egypt, where they will be strangers "in a land that is not theirs. . . Then in the fourth generation they will return here [to Canaan]" (Genesis 15:13–16).

Later, in another visitation, the Lord told Abraham: "No longer shall your name be called Abram, But your name will be called Abraham; For I have made you the father of a multitude of nations." He also instructed him: "Every male among you shall be circumcised. You shall be circumcised in the flesh of your foreskin, and it shall be the sign of the covenant between Me and you." This command, which Abraham carried out, forged another link between the Hebrew tribe and Egypt, for, until that moment in history, only Egyptians among the eastern nations had adopted the custom of circumcision. At the same time, Sarah's name also was changed. God said to Abraham: "As for Sarai your wife, you shall not call her name Sarai, Sarah shall be her name. I will bless her, and indeed I will give you a son by her. Then I will bless her, and she shall be a mother of nations; kings of peoples will come from her." So Isaac's descendants are promised to inherit the borders of the Egyptian Empire that existed at the time of the Eighteenth Dynasty, "From the river of Egypt as far as the great river, the river Euphrates" (Genesis 15:18).

A short time after the birth of Isaac, the Bible gives the account of a very strange event. According to Genesis 22:9–12, Abraham took Isaac to the top of a mountain where he proposed to sacrifice him as a burnt offering, until the Lord intervened. This curious episode shows how Abraham built an altar, placed the bound Isaac upon it and was about to slaughter him with a knife as a sacrifice, when the voice of the Lord cried out from heaven: "Do not stretch out your hand against the lad."

After his mother's death, when Isaac grew to manhood, he took a wife, Rebekah, who became pregnant with twins, both boys. The first to be born was named Esau, the second Jacob. Being the first-born, Esau is said to have had a birthright, which he later sold to his younger brother Jacob for some meal of "red pottage." With the help of Rebekah his mother, Jacob also received his father's blessing (of the birthright), which should have gone to Esau his firstborn. Fearing for his life, Rebekah advised Jacob to leave the family dwelling in Canaan and go to her bother Laban who lives in Haran in northern Mesopotamia. There, Jacob marries two of his uncle's daughters, as well as their two maids, and has twelve sons with them. Eventually, after many years in Haran, Jacob decides to return to Canaan and makes up with Esau his brother.

From this moment on, Jacob seems to have replaced Abraham as the head of the Hebrew tribe, and was given a new title "Israel," which was later adopted by a whole nation. As we have been told that Abraham's descendants will return to Egypt where they will dwell until the fourth generation, we are now introduced to a boy from Abraham's third generation who is destined to change the tribe's status forever. This was Joseph, the eleventh son of Jacob, from his beloved wife Rachel.

Jacob loved Joseph more than any of his other sons and made him a coat with many colors, an act that elicits much jealousy from Joseph's ten older half-brothers. As he did little to ingratiate himself to his brothers, while at the same time reporting their activities to his father, he alienated himself even more from them. Moreover, Joseph told his family about two dreams he had, which he interpreted as meaning that one day he will be the ruler over his family.

At last, his jealous brothers decide to get rid of Joseph by selling him to a Midianite trade caravan going down to Egypt, while reporting to their father that he was killed by a wild animal. When they arrive to Egypt, the Midianites sold young Joseph as a slave to Potiphar, one of Pharaoh's officials, who treated him well and made him supervisor over his house. However when Joseph refused to sleep with Potiphar's wife, she accused him of attempting to rape her, which landed him in prison.

While in prison, Joseph meets two inmates, Pharaoh's former butler and former baker, each of whom had a dream. Joseph interprets their dreams, predicting that in three days the baker would be executed while the butler will be restored to Pharaoh's service. Joseph then asks the butler to remember him when he returns to Pharaoh's service. Nevertheless, although Joseph's interpretation of their dreams proved to be right, the butler forgets his promise to Joseph until, after two years, when Pharaoh himself had some disturbing dreams. Pharaoh ordered Joseph to be brought from prison to interpret his dreams at the royal residence. In his interpretation, Joseph told Pharaoh that Egypt will have seven years of great abundance through the land, to be followed by seven years of famine. It was then that Pharaoh, who became pleased with the interpretation of his dreams, appointed Joseph to be one of his ministers.

About twenty years after he had been sold as a slave in Egypt, while Joseph was supervising the distribution of the fruits of the land of Egypt, a famine hit the land in Canaan, and Jacob sent his ten sons to buy corn in Egypt. Joseph recognized his brothers, while they were deceived by his Egyptian appearance. At the beginning he concealed his true identity from his brothers, then later he revealed himself to them and asked Pharaoh to allow his family to come and live in Egypt. Although Pharaoh gave his consent, nevertheless he did not allow the tribe of Israel, which consisted of seventy men, to dwell in the Nile Valley for the Israelites were shepherds and because shepherds had been looked upon as "an abomination" to Egyptians since the country's long occupation and rule of the eastern Delta by the pastoralist Hyksos that preceded the foundation of the Eighteenth Dynasty. Instead they were given land at Goshen, at the border in northern Sinai, to the east of the Nile Delta, which by biblical tradition was remote from the seat of Pharaoh's power.

When Jacob died some years later, Joseph ordered the physicians to embalm his father according to Egyptian traditions, and went up to Canaan to bury Jacob there. However, when Joseph himself died some years later, he was mummified and buried in Egypt.

Immediately after Joseph's death, which is reported in the very last verse of the Book of Genesis, the following Book of Exodus reports that: "Now a new king arose over Egypt, who did not know Joseph. He said to his people, 'Behold, the people of sons of Israel are more and mightier than we. Come, let us deal wisely with them, or else they will multiply and in the event of war, they will also join themselves to those who hate us, and fight against us and depart from the land'" (Exodus 1:8–10).

It was this new Pharaoh, who didn't know Joseph, who enslaved the Children of Israel by putting them to hard labor: "And they built for Pharaoh storage cities, Pithom and Raamses. . . . And they made their lives bitter with hard labor in mortar and bricks" (Exodus 1:11, 14). Pharaoh also ordered two midwives that all male children born to the Hebrew tribe should be killed. Yet the midwives failed to carry out Pharaoh's orders, whereupon he issued a further order that all male children born to the Israelites in Egypt were to be cast into the river.

With the second chapter of the Book of Exodus we come to the story of Moses: his birth, his slaying of an Egyptian that caused him to flee from the royal residence to Sinai, his marriage, and his eventual return to lead the Israelites in their Exodus.

Moses was born, we are told, to a man of the house of Levi and a daughter of Levi, whose name is given later as Jochebed. In face of the threat to all newly-born male Israelite children, Jochebed kept her son in hiding for three months. Then, unable to conceal him any longer, she hid him among the reeds along the banks of the Nile in a papyrus basket coated with pitch and tar. Pharaoh's daughter saw the basket when she went down to the river to bathe and sent a slave girl to fetch it. When she opened the basket the baby was crying and she felt sorry for him. "This is one of the Hebrew babies," she said.

Here we learn that Moses already had an elder sister called Miriam, who had watched these events from a distance. She now approached and said the Pharaoh's daughter: "Shall I go and call a nurse for you from the Hebrew women that she may nurse the child for you?" When this suggestion proved acceptable, the sister summoned her mother, who agreed to nurse her own baby in return for payment. Later, when the child grew older, she took him back to Pharaoh's daughter, who adopted him as her son and only now, we learn, gave him the name of Moses, her choice being explained by the laconic phrase "because I drew him out of the water."

The Book of Exodus does not provide any more details of Moses's childhood. We next hear of him when he had already grown up. He went out one day to watch the Hebrews at their forced labor, came across an Egyptian beating a Hebrew, slew the Egyptian, and hid his body in the sand. On learning that news of this episode had reached Pharaoh's ears, Moses fled to Midian in south Sinai to avoid execution.

There, while he was resting by a well, the seven daughters of the priest of Midian arrived on the scene to water their father's flock of sheep. Shortly afterward, some shepherds appeared and tried to drive the daughters away, but Moses came to their rescue. When Reu'el, their father, knew about this event, he asked his daughters to invite Moses to have a meal with them. This invitation proved to be the start of a protracted stay. Moses became a permanent guest in the house of the priest, who gave him one of his daughters, Zipporah, in marriage, and she bore Moses a son, whom he named Gershon.

Many years later, while Moses was looking after the flock of his father-in-law at Mount Horeb in Sinai, the Lord appeared to him in a flame of fire in the middle of a bush. The Lord then spoke to him, and instructed him to go back to Egypt to get the Israelites out, and told him that all those who wished to kill him are already dead. The Lord also asked Aaron, brother of Moses, to come and meet him in Sinai, and they went together to see the Israelite elders to inform them about the Lord's instructions.

The two brothers then went to see Pharaoh, demanding that he should let the Hebrew tribe go. When Pharaoh refused their demand, God sent a series of plagues upon Egypt, the final one, slaying the first-born among the Egyptians while passing over the firstborn among the Israelites, became the origin of the Passover night. This was followed by the most important account in the Bible, and the single most significant event in the history of the Israelites: the Exodus. The term "Exodus" here refers to the Israelites' departure, as it is described in the Book of Exodus. Thus the Israelites came to Egypt as a small Hebrew tribe but, through the Exodus, they became a nation, the people of God.

The Exodus began, from Ramses to Succoth, when 600,000 men plus their dependents are said to have left the country that had been their home for 430 years. From Succoth the Israelites made their way to Eltham where they camped before setting off on their journey across the wilderness to the Sea of Reeds. Nevertheless, instead of following the Way of Horus, that links Egypt with Canaan "the way of the land of the Philistines," the Israelites went "through the way of the wilderness of the Red Sea."

Back in Egypt, Pharaoh had second thoughts about his decision to let his former unwilling slaves to depart, and mounted an expedition with his chariots and troops to recapture them. They came upon the Israelites on the shores of the Red Sea, apparently trapped between the water and the pursuing Egyptians. Naturally terrified, they protested to Moses: "Is it because there are no graves in Egypt that you have taken us away to die in the desert?" However, Moses used his staff and the Lord divided the waters of the Red Sea, permitting the Israelites to pass through, allowing them a miraculous escape. When the Egyptians eventually set out in pursuit, the water flowed back over them and they were drowned to a man.

From the Red Sea, the Israelites made their way into the desert, and eventually reached Mount Sinai, where God gave Moses the Ten Commandments and made a covenant with the Children of Israel: they are to keep his Torah (law), and in return he will be their God and give them the land of Canaan. However, when Moses began to lead the Israelites in their journey through the wilderness to the land of Canaan,

Fig. 1.1. Mount Sinai. Photo courtesy of Ahmed Osman.

they began murmuring against him demanding the return to Egypt. So God declared that they should now wander for forty years in the wilderness of Sinai until the entire generation who rebelled against Moses will perish, and only the new generation will be allowed to enter the Promised Land. Moses himself was also forbidden from entering Canaan, and he died when he was 120 years old, and was buried in Moab, to the east of the Dead Sea.

2

WHO WROTE THE EXODUS STORY?

The Israelites' Exodus from Egypt, as it is described in the Bible, was taken to represent a true historical account for more than 2,000 years. Traditionally thought to be written by Moses, the Exodus story was believed to be the inspired word of God given to his prophet. Nevertheless, the question of how the Bible story has come down to us from the time of Moses has been the subject of continuing debate. People felt that the narration included a number of accounts coming from different sources. They also recognized that some parts of the story must have come from other authors and belonged to different times. For all these points, which were raised concerning the origins of the Pentateuch, people looked to the Church of Rome for their interpretation and guidance to help them understand these issues.

This situation changed after the Protestant Reformation in the sixteenth century, which challenged the authority of Rome as the only interpreter of the scriptures. Scholars of the Enlightenment, who promoted science and intellectual interchange, soon entered the scene of biblical scholarship. They started to point to long lists of inconsistencies, contradictions, and anachronisms in the Pentateuch. As a result, Western philosophers began to challenge the accuracy of the Bible, rejecting miracles and advocating reason in place of revelation. In England, Thomas Hobbes (1588–1670), the philosopher who developed some of the fundamentals of European liberal thought, noticed some textual discrepancies and suggested that Moses could not have written the Pentateuch alone. Twenty years later, Baruch de Spinoza (1632–1677), the Dutch pantheistic-rationalist, went further, completely rejecting the Mosaic authorship of the Pentateuch and denying the possibility of divine revelation. This new liberal movement rejected the idea of God's revelation and regarded the Bible as an ordinary piece of literature, rather than a divinely inspired text. When they examined it as an ordinary literary text, biblical scholars began to realize that the first five books of the Bible are actually composite works, redacted from different sources.

It was in the eighteenth century, however, that biblical source criticism originated with the work of Jean Astruc, who adapted the methods already used for investigating classical texts, to his investigation into the sources of the Book of Genesis. Although the House of Astruc had a medieval Jewish origin, Jean's father was a Protestant minister who converted to Catholicism. Jean was educated at Montpellier, one of the great schools of medicine in early modern Europe, where he also became a teacher before moving to the University of Paris. In 1753 Jean Astruc anonymously published a work entitled *Conjectures,* where he proposed that the Book of Genesis can be divided, based on the name for God used in different sections. As he noticed that some portions utilize Elohim as the name for God, while others use Jehovah (Yahweh), one identified the presence of Elohistic sections from the hand of one source, and Jehovistic sections from the hand of another source. Accordingly, Astruc suggested that Moses must have compiled the first five books of the Old Testament from two sources that had been transmitted over several centuries, either orally or in written form, and reassembled the ancient memories so as to furnish a continuous narrative, an approach that is called documentary hypothesis. Astruc found four documents in Genesis, which he arranged in four columns, declaring that this was how Moses had originally written his book, and that a later writer had combined them into a single work, creating the repetitions and inconsistencies that Hobbes, Spinoza, and others had noted.

About four generations later came Thomas Paine, a British-American revolutionary author who participated in both the American War of Independence and the French Revolution. Paine became one of the top Founding Fathers of the United States of America who signed the Declaration of Independence, together with people like George Washington and Benjamin Franklin. Paine published a pamphlet called *The Age of Reason* in 1794, 1795, and 1807 in which he saw the Bible as an ordinary piece of literature, rather than a divinely inspired word of God, rejecting miracles and advocating reason. Although the British government prosecuted printers and booksellers who tried to publish it in Britain, this book became very popular in the United States and Paine's ideas inspired many British freethinkers of the nineteenth and twentieth centuries. Those thinkers of the Enlightenment who embraced Isaac Newton's views of the universe demanded that all things, including God, should be examined according to the laws of nature. As miracles had to be tested before being validated, they rejected the accounts laid out in the Bible of God's miracles, arguing that miracles are not necessary to prove the existence of God.

In this new intellectual climate of freethinking and scientific approach, Astruc's ideas about the multiple origin of the Pentateuch were developed, chiefly in Germany, in the first half of the nineteenth century. Here biblical scholars became able to identify, not two, but four different sources behind the contents of the Pentateuch. These scholars were followed by K. H. Graf, who suggested in 1865 that the sections using the name Elohim, then assumed to be the earliest of the sources, were in fact from the later document, compiled at the time of Ezra the priest in the fifth century BCE, when Jewish scholars returned from Babylon to Jerusalem. This attempt by Graf to assign dates to the different documents started a new branch of study known as historical criticism. As a result, Bible scholars started to use the way a text is written—changes in style, vocabulary, repetitions and the like—to determine the different sources that were used by a biblical author and the date when it was written. Before the historical reliability of the biblical narratives of the Exodus can be judged, they needed to know as much as possible about how the various accounts were written, who wrote them, why they were written, and the sources of information available to their authors. The "historical-critical method," in which the text itself is subjected to rigorous internal analysis, became one of the ways to check the reliability of these accounts. In addition, they started to compare the biblical narratives to other ancient texts.

The final development of the German school's work was left to a man of wide spiritual vision, Julius Wellhausen (1844–1918), a biblical scholar and orientalist whose brilliant and penetrating mind led him to a prominent position in the field of Old Testament criticism. He is best known for his *Prolegomena to the History of Israel,* published in 1883, in which he advanced a definitive formulation of the documentary hypothesis, arguing that the Pentateuch had its origins in a redaction of four originally independent texts dating from several centuries after the time of Moses, their traditional author. Wellhausen's contribution was to put a historical date to the development of these books. Like Darwin, Wellhausen adopted the Hegelian idea of evolution and developed Graf's theories to what he thought were their natural conclusion. He regarded the Pentateuch as being composed of four main sources:

1. A Jehovistic source (J), dating from the ninth century BCE, and an Elohistic document (E), dating from the eighth century BCE.
2. The book of Deuteronomy (D), to be regarded as a separate source, dating from the seventh century BCE.
3. A priestly source (P), dating from about the fifth century BCE.
4. The work of an editor who revised and edited the entire collection around the second century BCE.

Wellhausan's views eventually found general acceptance and, since the latter part of the nineteenth century, almost all biblical scholars have come to agree that Moses did not write the first five books of the Bible. Instead, an agreement has developed in support of the theory that the Pentateuch was formed by weaving together four distinct documents, or sources, that were written down in different stages between the tenth century BCE and the sixth or fifth centuries at the time of the Babylonian Exile. However, since the twentieth century, some scholars saw even more hands at work in the Pentateuch, ascribing them to later periods than Wellhausen had proposed.

This brief outline of the development of biblical criticism makes it clear that the story of the Exodus as it has come down to us in the first five books of the Old Testament should be approached with a mixture of caution and common sense. One must make allowances for the fact that these stories were originally handed down over several centuries by word-of-mouth, with the inevitable distortions, and possible accretions that this would involve; that priests and editors have made their contribution to the text we know today; that translators have inserted interpolations, based on their own concept of morality; the inherent difficulties of translation itself and the fact that the language used in biblical times was vastly different from the language we use today.

The consensus among biblical scholars today is that there was never an exodus of the proportions described in the Bible and that the story is best seen as theology, a story illustrating how the God of Israel acted to save and strengthen his chosen people, and not as history. The view of modern biblical scholarship is that the improbability of the Exodus story originates because it was written not as history, but to demonstrate God's purpose and deeds with his Chosen People, Israel.

3

EGYPT REMEMBERS

As the biblical story of the Israelites' Descent and Exodus speaks about some important events that took place in Egypt, we should expect to find records of these events in Egyptian sources. The seven years of famine predicted by Joseph, the arrival of his father Jacob with his Hebrew family from Canaan, the great plagues of Moses, the death of Egypt's firstborn including Pharaoh's first son, and the drowning of Pharaoh himself in the Red Sea; all these events were worth mentioning by the scribes who usually kept detailed records of daily life. On the other hand, although some Hebrews are known to have been living in Egypt since the time of Thutmose III (1490–1468 BCE) working as laborers for the state, Israel became a special tribe since it had connection with the ruling Pharaoh, who appointed Joseph as his minister and brought Moses up in his royal palace. However, we find not even one contemporary inscription from the relevant period that records any of these events. Nevertheless, in spite of this silence, the name of Israel has been found inscribed on one of the pharaonic stelae, although with no connection either to Moses or the Exodus.

In 1896 W. M. Flinders Petrie, the British archaeologist, discovered a granite stele in the funerary temple of Amenhotep III (1405–1367 BCE) to the west of Thebes, which includes the name of "Israel." The stele, which had originally belonged to Amenhotep III and bore a text of his, was later usurped by Merenptah (1224–1214 BCE), who recorded on the other side the story of his victory over an invading Libyan tribal coalition. Now in the Cairo Museum, this stele has come to be known as the Israel Stele because it includes the first, and only, known mention of Israel in an Egyptian text.

In Year 5 of Merenptah, son and successor of Ramses II of the third king of the Nineteenth Dynasty, Egypt was invaded from the west by a tribal confederation, which included some Libyan elements, as well as five groups who came from the Greek islands. They entered the western delta with their women, children, and cattle, clearly intending permanent settlement, and attacked the cities of Memphis and Heliopolis in Lower Egypt. On learning of this threat, Merenptah sent his army, which met the invaders in the western delta, and defeated them in a matter of a few hours. After giving the details of this conflict, the stele concludes with a statement of twelve lines, confirming the submission of some foreign lands in Canaan to Egypt, including a statement that "Israel is laid waste, his seed is not." However, although the Merenptah stele locates the Israelites in Canaan around 1219 BCE, it has no mention of them having previously been living in Egypt or departing from it in an exodus under Moses.

This complete silence of official Egyptian records was broken by later Egyptian historians, who seem to have known many details about Moses and his Exodus. While contemporary pharaonic authorities seem to have deliberately suppressed the mention of Moses and his followers in their records, for more than ten centuries popular traditions kept the story of the man whom Egyptians regarded as a divine being, before it was later recorded by Egyptian priests. Under the Macedonian Ptolemaic Dynasty, which ruled Egypt after the death of Alexander the Great in 323 BCE, Egyptian historians made sure to include the story of Moses and his exodus in their historical accounts. When Ptolemy II, Philadelphus, asked Manetho, the third-century BCE Egyptian priest and historian, to write the history of Egypt in Greek to be placed in the Library of Alexandria, he included the story of Moses in his *Egyptiaca*. Manetho was one of the early Egyptians who wrote about his country in Greek, assembling information already existing in the ancient Egyptian records, including tales he found in the temple library, made up of popular stories that had initially been transmitted orally before being set down in writing. Although Manetho's original text was lost, some quotations from it have been preserved mainly by the first-century CE Jewish historian Flavius Josephus, as well as the Christian chronographers Sextus Julius Africanus of the third century and Eusebius of the fourth century, and in isolated passages in Plutarch and other classical writers. Manetho gave a complete history of the thirty-one royal dynasties that ruled Egypt from the time of Menes around 3100 BCE to Alexander the Great in 332 BCE, accompanied by short notes on outstanding kings and important events. Although there are some differences between these sources quoting Manetho, they all agree on these main points:

- Moses was an Egyptian and not a Hebrew.
- Moses lived at the time of Amenhotep III and his son Akhenaten (1405–1367 BCE).
- The Israelites' Exodus took place in the reign of a succeeding king whose name was Ramses.

According to Josephus, in his book *Against Apion,* Alexandria had become a main center for the Jews during the time of the Ptolemaic kings. They enjoyed both Alexandrian citizenship and the city's "finest residential quarter" by the sea. These Alexandrian Jews were naturally interested in Manetho's accounts of their ancient links with Egypt, which became a subject of debate between Jewish and Egyptian scholars. However, Josephus complains about Manetho and some other Egyptian historians

> who regard that man (Moses) as remarkable, indeed divine, wish to claim him as one of themselves (an Egyptian) while making the incredible and calumnious assertion that he was one of the priests expelled from Heliopolis for leprosy.[1]

Commenting on Manetho's account of Moses, Josephus tells us that

Under the pretext of recording fables and current reports about the
Jews, he (Manetho) took the liberty of introducing some incredible
tales, wishing to represent us (the Jews) as mixed up with a crowd
of Egyptian lepers and others, who for various maladies were con-
demned, as he asserts, to banishment from the country. Inventing
a king named Amenophis, an imaginary person, the date of whose
reign he consequently did not venture to fix. . . . This king, he states,
wishing to be granted a vision of the gods, communicated his desire
to his namesake, Amenophis, son of Paapis (Habu), whose wisdom
and knowledge of the future were regarded as marks of divinity. This
namesake replied that he would be able to see the gods if he purged
the entire country of lepers and other polluted persons. Delighted
at hearing this, the king collected all the maimed people in Egypt,
numbering 80,000 and sent them to work in the stone-quarries on
the east of the Nile, segregated from the rest of the Egyptians. They
included, he adds, some of the learned priests, who were afflicted
with leprosy. Then this wise seer Amenophis was seized with a fear
that he would draw down the wrath of the gods on himself and the
king if the violence done to these men were detected; and he added
a prediction that the polluted people would find certain allies who
would become masters of Egypt for thirteen years. He did not venture to tell this himself to the king, but left a complete statement
in writing, and then put an end to himself. The king was greatly
disheartened.[2]

Josephus was wrong in saying that Manetho invented a king named
Amenophis who communicated his desire to his namesake, Amenophis,
son of Paapis. This king has been identified as Amenhotep III, ninth
king of the Eighteenth Dynasty, while his namesake, Amenhotep son
of Habu, is known to have started his career under Amenhotep III as
an Inferior Royal Scribe, then promoted to be a Superior Royal Scribe,
and finally reached the position of Minister of all Public Works. The
son of Habu lived to be at least eighty and later became a kind of a

saint whose cult was reported as late as Roman times. On the other hand, Manetho's description of the rebels as being lepers and polluted people should not be taken literally to mean that they were suffering from some form of physical maladies, the sense here being that they were impure because of their denial of Egyptian religious beliefs.

Josephus proceeds quoting Manetho:

> When the men in the stone-quarries had continued long in misery, the king acceded to their request to assign them for habitation and protection the abandoned city of the shepherds (Hyksos), called Auaris (Avaris), and according to an ancient theological tradition dedicated to Typhon (Seth). Thither they went, and, having now a place to serve as a base for revolt, they appointed as their leader one of the priests of Heliopolis called Osarseph, and swore to obey all his orders.[3]

Although here Josephus gives the name of the rebel leader as Osarseph, it has been noted that this name looks like a transformation of Joseph, the Egyptian god of the dead Osiris being substituted for the first syllable, which would indicate "the already deceased Joseph." Chaeremon, the first-century librarian of Alexandria, gives the names of two rebel leaders, Moses and Peteseph (Joseph), in his *History*.[4] Thus Chemeron associates Moses with Joseph, who is supposed to have died some time before. Meanwhile, Josephus accused Apion, another Egyptian historian who wrote a *History of Egypt* in five books, of lying about the Jews, claiming that they were Egyptians by race, as he states in the third book of his *History*.

> Moses, as I have heard from old people in Egypt, was a native of Heliopolis, who, being pledged to the customs of his country, erected prayer-houses, open to the air, in the various precincts of the city, all facing eastwards; such being the orientation also of Heliopolis. . . . Apion . . . tells us elsewhere that Moses went up into the mountain called Sinai, which lies between Egypt and Arabia, remained in concealment there for forty days, and then descended and gave the Jews their laws.[5]

Josephus goes on to say that in the rebel leader's first law, he ordained that his followers should not worship the Egyptian gods nor abstain from the flesh of any of the animals held in special reverence in Egypt, but should kill and consume them all, and that they should have no connection with any save members of their own confederacy. After laying down these and a multitude of other laws, absolutely opposed to Egyptian customs, he ordered all hands to repair the walls of Avaris and make ready for war with King Amenophis. The rebel leader (Moses) then sent an embassy to the shepherds, inviting them to join him in his city and join him in an expedition against King Amenophis.

Although Josephus states that the shepherds who were invited by Moses were the Hyksos who had been driven out of Egypt by Ahmose about a century and a half earlier, Chaeremon states that there were some shepherds left in Pelusium in North Sinai by King Amenophis, who had refused them permission to cross the Egyptian frontier. These shepherds happily accepted the invitation, and set off to join the rebels in their city of Avaris. As the new alliance started to march against Egypt, Amenophis fled to Ethiopia (Nubia) whose king was under obligation to him and at his service, leaving his pregnant wife behind to give birth in hiding. Before leaving, however, Amenophis sent for the sacred animals, which were held in most reverence in the temples, and instructed the priests to conceal the images of the gods as securely as possible. In Nubia, Amenophis remained in exile for thirteen years, which confirmed the prediction of the son of Habu. During these years, the rebels treated the inhabitants in so sacrilegious a manner that the regime of the shepherds (Hyksos) seemed like a golden age to those who now beheld the impieties of their present enemies. Not only did they set cities and villages on fire, not only did they pillage the temples and mutilate the images of the gods, but, not content with that, they habitually used the very sanctuaries as kitchens for roasting the venerated sacred animals, forced the priests and prophets to slaughter them and cut their throats, and then turned them out naked. During these thirteen years also, according to Manetho's story as reported by Josephus, Amenhotep's wife, whom he had left in hiding, gave birth to a son named Ramses, "who, on reaching manhood, drove the Jews (Egyptian rebels and shepherds), to the number of about 200,000, into Syria (the Levant), and brought home his father Amenophis from Ethiopia."[6]

As we can see, although contemporary Egyptian official records kept their silence about the account of Moses and the Israelite Exodus, popular memory of Egypt preserved the story of these events, which had been transmitted orally for many centuries before it was put down in writing. These traditions knew about Moses and Joseph and also knew about the shepherds who lived at the borders and were not allowed to enter the Nile Valley.

Manetho could not have invented this information, as he could only rely on the records he found in the temple scrolls. Neither could he have been influenced by the stories of the Bible, as the Torah was only translated from Hebrew to Greek some time after he had composed his *Egyptiaca*. As Donald B. Redford, the Canadian Egyptologist, has remarked:

> What he (Manetho) found in the temple library in the form of a duly authorized text he incorporated in his history; and, conversely, we may with confidence postulate for the material in his history a written source found in the temple library, and nothing more.[7]

On the other hand, Manetho's dating of the religious rebellion to the time of Amenhotep III assures us that he was giving a real historical account. For it was during the reign that Amenhotep's son and coregent, Akhenaten, abandoned traditional Egyptian polytheism and introduced a monotheistic worship centered on the Aten. Akhenaten, like the rebel leader, also erected his new temples open to the air facing eastward; in the same way as the orientation of Heliopolis. This similarity between Akhenaten and the rebel leader persuaded Donald Redford to recognize Manetho's Osarseph story as the events of the Amarna religious revolution, first remembered orally and later set down in writing, "a number of later independent historians, including Manetho, date Moses and the bondage to the Amarna period? Surely it is self-evident that the monotheistic preaching at Mount Sinai is to be traced back ultimately to the teachings of Akhenaten."[8] Redford also confirms that: "The figure of Osarseph/Moses is clearly modeled on the historic memory of Akhenaten. He is credited with interdicting the worship of all the gods and, in Apion, of championing a form of worship which used open-air temples oriented east, exactly like the Aten temples of Amarna."[9]

As for the starting point of the Exodus, while the biblical account gives the city's name as Ramses, Manetho gives the name of another location: Avaris. Avaris was a fortified city at the borders of the Nile Delta and Sinai, the starting point of the road to Canaan, which had been occupied by the Asiatic kings, known as Hyksos, who ruled Egypt from about 1783 BCE to 1550 BCE, when they were driven out by Ahmose I.

As for the Pharaoh of the Exodus, while the Bible does not mention the name of this king, Manetho calls him Ramses. Nevertheless, as the confused popular memory makes Ramses, who was of nonroyal birth, a son of Amenhotep III, Ramses I ruled after the death of Horemheb, the last king of the Eighteenth Dynasty, and established his own Nineteenth Dynasty. Ramses was already an old man when he came to the throne, and ruled for less than two years; he could have been born under Amenhotep III, who died about sixty years earlier.

Now that the time when Moses lived in Egypt was identified under Amenhotep III, the starting point of the Exodus located at Avaris, and the Pharaoh of the Exodus identified as Ramses I, it seemed like the road had already been opened to start looking for historical and archaeological evidence to confirm this account. Scholars, however, did not follow this route of investigation, and went on looking for the evidence in other times and different locations. Thanks to Flavius Josephus, who wrongly identified the Hebrew tribe not with the shepherds who were already living in Egypt, but with the Hyksos rulers who had left the country more than a century earlier, modern scholars dismissed Manetho's account as unhistorical.

4

HYKSOS OR ISRAELITES

In contrast to the silence of contemporary Egyptian records on the story of Moses and the Exodus, Manetho's Osarseph account, surprisingly, confirms the historicity of the main biblical account. It confirms that the shepherds (who followed Moses) were living at the Sinai borders, and were not allowed to enter the Valley of the Nile, in complete agreement with Genesis 46:34, "ye may dwell in the land of Goshen; for every shepherd is an abomination unto the Egyptians." The Alexandrian Egyptian historians mention Moses by name, recognizing his relation with Joseph, exactly as the Bible says. They present Moses as a religious rebel, who rejected the worship of sacred Egyptian gods, and went to Mount Sinai to receive the Law, in complete agreement with the Bible. It was Moses also, according to Egyptian historians, who led his followers, Egyptians and shepherds, in an Exodus out of Egypt, in the time of a Pharaoh called Ramses. Nevertheless Josephus, ignoring all these points of similarity between the Bible and Egyptian accounts, insisted on regarding the Hyksos, who left the country about two centuries earlier, as being the same people as the Israelites. Josephus confirmed that the Hyksos were the patriarchal Jews, equating their appearance in Egypt with the Joseph story in Genesis and their subsequent expulsion with the biblical tale of Exodus.

Except for the fact that both Hyksos and the Israelites were Semites who came to Egypt from the east then left some time later, no element of the Bible can be found in the Hyksos account.

> Manetho has thus furnished us with evidence from Egyptian literature on two most important points: first that we (the Jews) came into Egypt from elsewhere, and secondly, that we left it at a date so remote in the past.[1]

In order to justify this unsupported conclusion, Josephus attempted to explain the word "Hyksos" to indicate that they were shepherds, in the same way as the Israelites.

> Their race bore the generic name of Hyesos (Hyksos), which means "king-shepherds." For *hyk* in the sacred language denotes "king," and *sos* in the common dialect means "shepherd" or, "shepherds"; the combined words from Hyesos.[2]

This explanation, however, was not accepted by Alan Gardiner, the British Egyptologist and linguist.

> This etymology he (Josephus) prefers because he believed . . . that the biblical story of the Israelite sojourn in Egypt and the subsequent Exodus had as its source the Hyksos occupation and later expulsion. In point of fact, although there are sound linguistic grounds for both etymologies, neither is the true one. The word Hyksos undoubtedly derives from the expression *hik-khase,* "chieftain of a foreign hill-country," which from the Middle Kingdom onward was used to designate Bedouin sheiks. Scarabs bearing this title, but with the word "countries" in the plural, are found with several undoubted Hyksos kings. . . . It is important to observe, however, that the term refers to the rulers alone, and not, as Josephus thought, to the entire race. Modern scholars have often erred in this matter, some even implying that the Hyksos were a particular race of invaders, who after conquering Syria and Palestine ultimately forced their way into Egypt. Nothing justifies such a view,

even though the actual words of Manetho might seem to support it. It is true enough that for some centuries past there had been a growing pressure of alien peoples downward into Syria, Hurrians from the Caspian region being among the first, these paving the way for the Hittites who followed from the northwest at the end of the sixteenth century. But of such movements there can have been no more than distant repercussions on the Egyptian border. The invasion of the delta by a specific new race is out of the question; one must think rather of an infiltration by Palestinians glad to find refuge in a more peaceful and fertile environment. . . . It is doubtless impossible to support the erroneous usage of the word Hyksos as though it referred to a special race, but it should be borne in mind that the Egyptians themselves usually employed for those unwelcomed intruders the term Amu, which we translate with rough accuracy as "Asiatics" and which had much earlier served to designate Palestinian captives or hirelings in Egypt as servants.[3]

When we try to find out the reason behind Josephus's rejection of the Osarseph account in favor of the Hyksos account to represent the Israelites, we realize that his main reason was the fact that Egyptian historians: "regard that man (Moses) as remarkable, indeed divine, wish to claim him as one of themselves."[4]

5

FREUD'S DREAM

About nineteen centuries after Josephus had rejected the Egyptian Moses, a modern Jewish scholar came to support Manetho's account. Sigmund Freud, one of the most influential thinkers of the twentieth century whose controversial theories have helped to reshape our modern culture, agreed with the Egyptian historian that Moses was an Egyptian, who lived during the time of Amenhotep III. Freud, the Jewish father of psychoanalysis, wrote in July 1934 a draft article of what would become the first part of his last book *Moses and Monotheism,* which was published initially in the German magazine *Imago* in 1937 under the headline "Moses an Egyptian." In this article Freud stated that: "Perhaps it seemed monstrous to imagine that the Man Moses could have been anything other than a Hebrew."[1] He stressed, however, that the objective truth could not be suppressed for national interest.

> To deny a people the man whom it praises as the greatest of its sons is not a deed to be undertaken light-heartedly—especially by one belonging to that people. No consideration, however, will move me to set aside truth in favor of supposed national interests. . . . The man Moses, the liberator of his people, who gave them their religion and their laws, belonged to an age so remote that the preliminary question arises whether he was an historical person or a legendary

figure. If he lived, his time was the thirteenth or fourteenth century BCE; we have no word of him but from the Holy Books and the written traditions of the Jews.[2]

Sigmund Freud was born on May 6, 1856, in Freiberg, a small town in Moravia, which was at the time part of Austria-Hungary. He came of a middle-class Jewish family and was the eldest child of his father's second wife. His father was a wool merchant who came under increasing commercial difficulties, which made him leave his hometown when Freud was just three years old, and later settle in Vienna, the city that was the capital of a huge empire. From his earliest years, Freud was an inquisitive and open-minded child. After finishing his early education at the age of seventeen, Freud decided to study medicine at the University of Vienna: "In my youth I felt an overpowering need to understand something of the riddles of the world in which we live and perhaps even to contribute something to their solution."[3] Following the first year at the university where he studied a variety of subjects, he concentrated on biology and physiology, before joining a Physiological Laboratory for six years. In 1881, after eight years of study, Freud took his medical degree and started working in the Vienna General Hospital. It was then, at the age of twenty-five, that he became engaged to be married to Martha Bernays, a German Jewish girl from Hamburg.

Although at the beginning he worked in various departments of the hospital, Freud soon came to concentrate on neuroanatomy, the anatomy of the nervous system. A turning point in his medical interest took place in 1885, when he went to Paris to work on nervous disease under Jean-Martin Charcot. Charcot was a French neurologist and professor of pathology, whose work greatly influenced the developing of psychology. When he returned to Vienna the following year, Freud set up his private practice as a consultant in nervous diseases, and got married at the same time. He established his consulting rooms in the same house where he lived, from 1891 until he left Vienna for London forty-seven years later.

While there is no indication that Sigmund Freud had any knowledge of either Manetho's account of the Egyptian Moses or of Josephus's rejection of this account, his conclusion was not built on historical evidence, but rather on a psychological investigation. In any case, Freud's views cannot be dismissed without examining the reasons that made him come to this conclusion.

In order to know the reason behind Sigmund Freud's conclusion that Moses was an Egyptian, we have to follow his research. Freud was interested to know how the human mind worked, and was able to discover the first instrument for the scientific examination of the human mind. He developed theories about the unconscious mind and the mechanism of repression, and he established the field of verbal psychotherapy for treating these cases through the use of psychoanalysis, which was a clinical method he created for curing psychopathology through dialogue between a patient and a psychoanalyst.

> The unconscious contents of the mind were found to consist wholly in the activity of conative trends—desires or wishes—which derive their energy directly from the primary physical instincts. They function quite regardless of any consideration other than of obtaining immediate satisfaction, and are thus liable to be out of step with those more conscious elements in the mind which are concerned with adaptation to reality and the avoidance of external dangers.[4]

Freud was also interested in the meaning of dreams from the time he was just a youth, when he used to retreat into the world of imagination. Later, in 1900 he published a fundamental work on *The Science of Dreams*.

> [H]is self-analysis led him to an inquiry into the nature of dreams. These turned out to be, like neurotic symptoms, the product of a conflict and a compromise between the primary unconscious impulses and the secondary conscious ones. By analyzing them into their elements it was therefore possible to infer their hidden unconscious contents; and, since dreams are common phenomena of almost universal occurrence, their interpretation turned out to be one of the most useful technical contrivances for penetrating the resistance of neurotic patients.[5]

Freud then tried to explain the psychological origins of religious beliefs in his study, *Obsessive Actions and Religious Practices,* which appeared in 1907. He saw religion as a belief that people want very much to be true, a largely unconscious neurotic response to repression. Freud regarded God as an illusion, based on the infantile need for a powerful, supernatural father figure. Religion, he believed, was only necessary for the development of earlier civilizations, to help people restrain their violent impulses, which can now be set aside in favor of reason and science.

Six years later, Freud employed the application of psychoanalysis to the fields of archaeology, anthropology, and the study of religion in a new book *Totem and Taboo.* The totem is the common ancestor of the clan; at the same time it is their guardian spirit and helper. While *taboo* has two contrasting meanings: the "sacred" or "consecrated" and the "dangerous" or "forbidden," which still plays a significant role in modern society. Freud believes that an original act of patricide—the killing and devouring of "the violent primal father" was remembered and reenacted as a "totem meal . . . mankind's earliest festival," which was "the beginning of so many things—of social organization, of moral restrictions and of religion."[6]

The German invasion of Austria in 1938 started the last phase of Freud's life, as well as the life of many Jews who were living in Vienna at the time. The Jewish Austrian population, about 300,000, had enjoyed a period of freedom and prosperity from the mid-nineteenth century. Vienna, where Freud lived with about two-thirds of the Austrian Jews, was also a center of Zionist thought, where Theodor Herzl, the father of Zionism, had lived a few doors away from the father of psychoanalysis. When Hitler annexed Austria on March 13, 1938, many Jews tried to emigrate out of the country. Soon the city of Vienna with its large Jewish population suffered from the intensified anti-Jewish measures imposed on the community. Sigmund Freud's publications were burned publicly in the street. Nevertheless, Freud decided to stay in Vienna under the threat of the violent anti-Semitism that followed. It was Ernest Jones, the British President of the International Psychoanalytic Association, who was able to persuade Freud to move to London in the early summer of 1938, only when his daughter Anna had been detained for interrogation by the Gestapo. It was then, in his new North London home at Hampstead, that Freud thought that the time had come for him to complete his work on *Moses and Monotheism,* which was published in March 1939, a few months before his death on September 23, 1939.

However, Freud's decision to publish *Moses and Monotheism* in London came at a time when the Jews were facing Nazi persecution in Germany and Austria, which soon after spread all over occupied Europe. This dangerous political atmosphere made a number of Jewish leaders disagree on Freud's insistence on publishing this book: they felt that some of his views, and in particular his claim that Moses had been murdered by his own followers in protest against the harshness of his monotheistic beliefs, could only add to the problems of the Jews, already facing a new harsh oppression by the Nazis. Abraham S. Yahuda, the American Jewish theologian and philologist, visited Freud at his new home in London, and begged him not to publish the book, but Freud insisted and felt it would provide a fitting climax to his distinguished life, and *Moses and Monotheism* made its first appearance in March 1939.

Freud, however, had no intension of harming the Jewish people; on the contrary he believed that by revealing what he thought to be the real historical Moses, he would relieve his people of their suffering. According to his biographer, Ernest Jones, Freud's Jewishness, although he was a secular Jew, contributed significantly to his work. Freud himself believed that being a Jew helped him to be free from dogmatic beliefs and made him more objective.

> There was the fact of having been born a Jew I owed two characteristics that had become indispensable to me in the difficult course of my life. Because I was a Jew, I found myself free from many prejudices which restricted others in the use of their intellect; and as a Jew, I was prepared to join the Opposition, and do that without agreement with the "compact majority."[7]

Even though he never really observed the rites and precepts of his religion, he felt himself to be Jewish and kept wondering why he was treated differently just because he was a Jew. In *An Autobiographical Study,* published in 1925, Freud recounts that "My parents were Jews, and I have remained a Jew myself."[8] In 1873, upon attending the University at Vienna, he first encountered anti-Semitism: "I found that I was expected to feel myself inferior and an alien because I was a Jew."[9] This feeling, however, did not stop him from regarding himself as a universal man who belonged to his time.

Although he became familiar with the Bible stories from an early age, even before he learned to read and write, Freud describes himself as "an author who is ignorant of the language of holy writ, who is completely estranged from the religion of his fathers—as well as from every other religion,"[10] but who remains "in his essential nature a Jew and who has no desire to alter that nature."[11] At the time, during the late nineteenth and the early twentieth centuries, there were three different views regarding the Jewish question: "Three Jewishly-conflicted German speakers changed the course of modern history." By the time the first, Karl Marx (the philosopher and economist who wrote *Capital* and *The Communist Manifesto*), had died in 1883, Sigmund Freud and Theodor Herzl were rising stars in their twenties; later, they came to be neighbors living but a few doors apart on a Vienna street. Whereas Herzl determined that solving the Jewish problem necessitated sovereignty and statehood, Marx and Freud were more concerned with what ailed universal man, offering solutions more ambitious than mere tinkering with political organization. For Marx, economic reality was the key determinant; but Freud understood the human instinct of aggression and self-destruction that was present regardless of the reigning political system.

How Freud's ideas fared is the subject of a new book by the Tel Aviv based psychoanalyst and historian Eran Rolnik, entitled *Freud in Zion.* The book's subtitle, *Psychoanalysis and the Making of Modern Jewish Identity,* is a bit of a tease.

> Nineteenth-century political Zionism understood the Diaspora as being mentally, physically, politically, and culturally injurious to a healthy Jewish life. Recovery could only come by its negation. By

contrast, in developing psychoanalysis Freud's goal was universal: to help people understand their drives, themselves, and thereby ameliorate emotional pain. Meanwhile, Freud's own concern was that anti-Semitic attitudes would tarnish the all-embracing message of psychoanalysis. He did not want his theories to be seen as commentary on the Jewish condition, writes Rolnik. Freud, after all, was thoroughly assimilated: the family celebrated a secular Christmas and Easter, not Passover. Nevertheless, he never considered conversion, perhaps because he came to view all religion as neurosis. . . . But Freud was put off by any hint of Jewish chauvinism. Hence his odd last book, *Moses and Monotheism* which, in Rolnik's view, was Freud's attempt to show that Jewish ethnicity and nationalism were not integral to its main gift to humanity.[12]

And although Freud lived on the same street in Vienna as Theodor Herzl, founder of political Zionism, for several years, Herzel's concept of redemption through political action ran contrary to Freud's rationalist commitment to the scientific analysis of dreams and the interpretation of the unconscious.

When he came to London, Freud tried to explain how this book haunted him for a long time: "I have not been able to efface the traces of the unusual way in which this book came to be written. In truth it has been written twice over. The first time was a few years ago in Vienna, where I did not believe in the possibility of publishing it. I decided to put it away, but it haunted me like an un-laid ghost, and I compromised by publishing two parts of the book independently in the periodical *Imago*. They were the psychoanalytical starting points of the whole book: *Moses an Egyptian* and the historical essay built on it "If Moses was an Egyptian."

The rest, which might give offence and was dangerous—namely, the application of my interpretation of religion—I kept back, as I thought, forever. Then in March 1938 came the unexpected German invasion. It forced me to leave my home, but it also freed me of the fear lest my publishing the book might cause psycho-analysis to be forbidden in a country where its practice was still allowed. No sooner had I arrived in England than I found the temptation of making my with-held knowledge accessible to the world irresistible, and so I started to rewrite the third part of my essay, to follow the two already published.[13]

In this book, his last, Freud explained how he tried to find the reason behind the anti-Jewish feeling, in the Jewish character itself.

Several years ago I started asking myself how the Jews acquired their particular character, and following my usual custom I went back to the earliest beginnings. I did not get far. I was astounded to find that already the first, so to speak, embryonic experience of the race, the influence of the man Moses and the exodus from Egypt, conditioned the entire further development up to the present day—like a regular trauma of early childhood in the case history of a neurotic individual. To begin with, there is the temporal conquest of magic thought; the rejection of mysticism, both of which can be traced back to Moses himself. . . . Moses was an Egyptian—probably an aristocrat—whom the legend was designed to turn into a Jew. . . . The deviation of the legend of Moses from all the others of its kind can be traced back to a special feature of his history. Whereas normally a hero, in the course of his life, rises above his humble beginnings, the heroic life of the man Moses began with his stepping down from his exalted position and descending to the level of the Children of Israel.[14]

Freud explained how the original story of Moses's birth could have been

almost all important civilized peoples have early on woven myths around and glorified in poetry their heroes, mythical kings and princes, founders of religions, of dynasties, empires and cities—in short their national heroes. Especially the history of their birth and of their early years is furnished with phantastic traits; the amazing similarity, nay, literal identity, of those tales, even if they refer to different, completely independent peoples, sometimes geographically far removed from one another, is well known and has struck many an investigator. . . . The hero is the son of parents of the highest station, most often the son of a king. His conception is impeded by difficulties, such as abstinence or temporary sterility; or else his parents practice intercourse in secret because of prohibitions or other external obstacles. During his mother's pregnancy or earlier an oracle or a dream warns the father of the child's birth as containing grave danger for his safety.

In consequence the father . . . gives orders for the new-born babe to be killed or exposed to extreme danger; in most cases the babe is placed in a casket and delivered to the waves. The child is then saved by animals or poor people, such as shepherds, and suckled by a female animal or a woman of humble birth. When full grown he rediscovers his noble parents after many strange adventures, wreaks vengeance on his father and, recognized by his people, attains fame and greatness.

The best known names in the series beginning with Sargon of Agade are Moses, Cyrus, and Romulus. But besides these Rank has enumerated many other heroes belonging to myth or poetry to whom the same youthful story attaches either in its entirety or in well recognizable parts, such as Oedipus, Karna, Paris, Telephos, Perseus, Heracles, Gilgamesh, Amphion, Zethos and others.[15]

He pointed out, however, that the story of Moses's birth and exposure differ from those of the other heroes and varies from them on one essential point. While in all other cases, the child is born to a royal family and brought up in a poor family, in the case of Moses the myth has been reversed to make him born to a humble Hebrew family and brought up by the pharaonic royal family.

It is very different in the case of Moses. Here the first family—usually so distinguished—is modest enough. He is a child of Jewish Levites. But the second family—the humble one in which, as a rule, heroes are brought up—is replaced by the royal house of Egypt. This divergence from the usual type has struck many research workers as strange.

Whereas in all other cases the hero rises above his humble beginnings as his life progresses, the heroic life of the man Moses began by descending from his eminence to the level of the children of Israel. This little investigation was undertaken in the hope of gaining from it a second, fresh argument for the suggestion that Moses was an Egyptian.[16]

Freud also demonstrated that the name of the Israelite leader, Moses, was not derived from Hebrew, as had been thought before, but was an Egyptian name, [M O S] "Mose," meaning "child," or "son." This is found in many Egyptian names: Ptahmose, Ramose (Ramses), Thutmose. Earlier in 1937 *Imago* had published an article by Freud under the title "If Moses was an Egyptian" in which he dealt with the question of why the Israelite leader, if actually Egyptian, should have passed on to his followers a monotheistic belief, rather than the classical ancient Egyptian plethora of gods and images. To answer this question, Freud found that the only Egyptian leader who rejected ancient Egyptian deities for a monotheistic belief was Akhenaten, son of Amenhotep III. Without being aware of Manetho's account, Freud came to the conclusion that Moses lived during the time of Amenhotep III. He found great similarity between the Aten religion introduced by Akhenaten, Amenhotep III's son, and the religious teaching attributed to Moses. For example, he wrote:

> The Jewish creed says: Schema Yisrael Adonai Elohenu Adonai Echod (Hear, O Israel, the Lord our God is one God). As the Egyptian letter t of Aten is equivalent of the Hebrew letter d, and the vowel e becomes o in Hebrew.

He went on to explain that this sentence from the Jewish creed could be translated as: "Hear, O Israel, our God Aten is the only God."

Later, when Freud published his book *Moses and Monotheism* in London in 1939, he suggested that the biblical Moses was one of

Akhenaten's high officials who, after the death of the king, selected the Hebrew tribe dwelling at Goshen to be his chosen people, and led them out in the Exodus.

Although response to Freud's book was delayed by the outbreak of World War II a few months after the publication, very few scholars accepted his historical explanation, while it was welcomed by much outraged condemnation as a malicious attack upon the very foundations of Jewish existence. Yerushalmi, an American professor of Jewish History, explains the reasons behind the Jewish rejection of the book.

> I presume that the bare plot . . . of Freud's *Moses* is, by now notorious. Monotheism is not of Jewish origin but an Egyptian discovery. The pharaoh Amenhotep IV established it as his state religion in the form of an exclusive worship of the sun-power, or Aten, thereafter calling himself Akhenaten. The Aten religion, according to Freud, was characterized by the exclusive belief in one God, the rejection of the anthropomorphism, magic, and sorcery, and the absolute denial of an afterlife. Upon Akhenaten's death, however, his great heresy was rapidly undone, and the Egyptians reverted to their old gods. Moses was not a Hebrew but an Egyptian priest or noble, and a fervent monotheist. In order to save the Aten religion from extinction he placed himself at the head of an oppressed Semitic tribe then living in Egypt, brought them forth from bondage, and created a new nation. He gave them an even more spiritualized, imageless form of monotheistic religion and, in order to set them apart, introduced the Egyptian custom of circumcision. But the crude mass of former slaves could not bear the severe demands of the new faith. In a mob revolt Moses was killed and the memory of the murder repressed. . . . However, over a period of centuries the submerged tradition of the true faith and its founder gathered sufficient force to reassert itself and emerge victorious. Yahweh was henceforth endowed with the universal and spiritual qualities of Moses's god, though the memory of Moses's murder remained repressed among the Jews, reemerging only in a very disguised form with the rise of Christianity.[17]

While Josephus had refused Manetho's Osarseph account because it makes Moses an Egyptian, Freud's argument makes him a follower of Akhenaten and claims that he was killed by his Israelite followers. As we shall see later, my own research proved that Moses was Akhenaten himself who had mixed Egyptian and Israelite blood, and that he was not killed by the Israelites.

6

HEBREWS, ISRAELITES, AND JEWS

Many authors in modern times, including specialized scholars, use the words "Hebrew," "Israelite," and "Jew" as if they are synonyms, all referring to the same people. This, however, is not true.

Hebrews: Were seminomadic groups that appeared in Canaan during the fifteenth and fourteenth centuries BCE, some of whom moved to Egypt and Mesopotamia. Abraham is described in the Book of Genesis as being a Hebrew, and this expression is also used in the first five books of the Bible to differentiate between the Israelites and both Egyptians and Philistines. The term "Hebrew" seems to have been used to designate groups of people who belonged to a particular social class and were engaged in harsh labor.

Israelites: Represent the Hebrew tribe of Jacob, who later received the title of Israel. Jacob and his family migrated to Egypt to join Joseph the Patriarch when he was working as a high official in the Egyptian pharaonic palace. So, although the Israelites were Hebrews, not all the Hebrews were Israelites. Moreover, from the time Jacob's descendants were freed by Moses, they were no longer referred to as Hebrews and became known only as Children of Israel, or Israelites.

Jews: The Old Testament never refers either to Moses or to any of the Israelites as being Jews. The Hebrew word for Jews, "Yahudi," originally meant "from the tribe of Judah," the fourth son of Jacob. However, this word was later used by Greek and Latin authors and by the Christian Church to indicate the people of Judaea as well as their religion. Following the Diaspora, the people themselves started to use this term for themselves and their religion. So Abraham was a Hebrew, Moses was an Israelite, and Freud was a Jew.

7

VELIKOVSKY'S MYTH

About six months after the publication of *Moses and Monotheism* in March 1939, Adolf Hitler started World War II by invading Poland on September 1, and Sigmund Freud died in London twenty-two days later. The outbreak of the war, which lasted about six years, delayed response to the bombshell that Freud had left behind. However, a few years after fighting had come to an end, Immanuel Velikovsky came to challenge Freud's claim that Moses was an Egyptian, a follower of Akhenaten. While Freud attempted to penetrate the human mind in order to interpret the ancient dream through the unconscious, Velikovsky relied on ancient myths to prove the historicity of the biblical chronology through miraculous events.

Immanuel Velikovsky was born in 1895 to a prosperous Jewish family in Vitebsk, Russia (now in Belarus). He studied Russian and mathematics at the Medvednikov Gymnasium in Moscow before traveling to Europe to study medicine at Montpellier in southern France and Edinburgh in Scotland. He returned to Moscow and completed his medical education at the age of twenty-six, then left again for Berlin where he became engaged in a project of preparing two volumes of scientific papers in Hebrew that became the cornerstone in the formation of the Jerusalem Hebrew University.

Following his marriage in 1923 to Elisheva Kramer, a young Jewish

Fig. 7.1. Immanuel Velikovsky.

violinist, the family moved to settle in Palestine where Velikovsky started his practice as a physician while studying psychoanalysis with Wilhelm Stekel, the first disciple of Freud. It was during these years also that he organized a cooperative Jewish kibbutz in the Negev desert called "Ruhama," which had been established in 1911 by a company set up by Russian Jews under the leadership of his father, Simon Velikovsky.

Fifteen years later, when Freud had published his book *Moses and Monotheism,* Velikovsky decided to leave Palestine for New York with the sole intention of refuting Freud's argument. Although initially he planned a book about Freud's dream interpretations and his heroes *Oedipus and Akhenaten,* he decided to delay this project, which was published later in 1960, and began to develop a radical catastrophic cosmology to prove that Moses and the Israelite Exodus preceded the time of Akhenaten by about five centuries. The result of his work was published in the book *Worlds in Collision* in 1950, which became very popular in the United States.

Later, when he wrote his memories, Velikovsky explained his motives behind writing this book.

By the beginning of April 1940 . . . I had with me the pages of a manuscript I had begun, *Freud and His Heroes*. Free from all other duties, I intended to finish and publish it in the United States. . . . This new manuscript . . . was inspired by Freud's last book, *Moses and Monotheism*. I disagreed with Freud and saw in the octogenarian a still-unresolved conflict with respect to his Jewish origin and his own father. I turned to his dreams to know more of him than his books could tell. I found that his own dreams, sixteen in number, interspersed among numerous dreams of his patients in his classic *The Interpretation of Dreams,* spoke of a language that was very clear but had meaning, which Freud did not comprehend, or did not reveal to his readers. All the dreams dealt with the problem of his Jewish origin, the tragic fate of his people, his deliberations on leaving the ranks of the persecuted for the sake of unhampered advancement or at least in order to free his children from the fate of underprivileged Jews in Christian and anti-Semitic Vienna. From this conflict, in which he struggled with himself, he emerged victorious in the last years before the turn of the century, about the time when, unknown and obscure, he wrote his book on dreams . . .

To reinterpret the dreams of the founder of modern dream interpretation was certain guarantee to a daring enterprise, but I used a method that carried a certain guarantee of objectivity. Besides, having found the same idea in all sixteen dreams, I believed, following Freud's premise, that "those ideas in the dream—thoughts, which are most important—are probably also those which recur most frequently." This interpretation of Freud's dreams would have constituted the part of the book dealing with the psychoanalyst himself. Other chapters were to deal with his heroes: Oedipus, Akhenaten, and Moses. A very unusual idea struck me when I studied the life of Akhenaten: it appeared to me that I had found the historical prototype of the Oedipus legend."[1]

Velikovsky, who met Freud on a few occasions in Vienna, was a passionate Zionist who believed that the best way to support the rights of the Jews to establish the state of Israel in Palestine, the Promised

Land, was to confirm the historicity of the Bible in its literal meaning. He realized that there was insufficient correlation in both written and archaeological sources between biblical and Egyptian histories. In order to confirm biblical chronology, Velikovsky claimed that the history of the ancient Near East, down to the time of Alexander the Great at the end of the fourth century BCE, was garbled. Relying on some ancient mythical tales that included accounts of natural catastrophes as well as catastrophic events in the Bible, Velikovsky proposed a revised chronology of ancient Egypt, synchronizing it with the biblical history of Israel. So, instead of looking for confirmation in historical and archaeological evidence, Velikovsky decided to find evidence in ancient myths to confirm the miraculous events of the biblical story, such as the Ten Plagues. In his book *Worlds in Collision,* Velikovsky used some ancient mythologies from different parts of the world to conclude that planet Earth had in the past experienced catastrophic close-contacts with other planets, such as Venus and Mars. He stated that around the fifteenth century BCE a comet, which he identifies as planet Venus, separated from Jupiter and passed near the Earth, changing its orbit and axis and causing innumerable catastrophes. These events, according to Velikovsky, caused upheaval upon the psyche of the Earth's inhabitants who experienced the calamities.

The plausibility of Velikovsky's theory, however, was rejected by the physics community who regarded the cosmic chain of events he proposed as contradicting the basic laws of physics. The fundamental criticism against the book from the astronomy community was that its celestial mechanics were irreconcilable with Newtonian celestial mechanics. Tim Callahan, religious editor of *Skeptic,* argued that the composition of the atmosphere of Venus is a complete disproof of Velikovsky's theory.

> Velikovsky's hypothesis stands or falls on Venus having a reducing atmosphere made up mainly of hydrocarbons. In fact, the atmosphere of Venus is made up mainly of carbon dioxide-carbon in its *oxidized* form, along with clouds of sulfuric acid. Therefore, it couldn't have carried such an atmosphere with it out of Jupiter, and

it couldn't be the source of hydrocarbons to react with oxygen in our atmosphere to produce carbohydrates. Velikovsky's hypothesis is falsified by the carbon dioxide atmosphere of Venus.[2]

Another astronomer, Philip Plait, relying on the presence of the moon, also rejected Velikovsky's hypothesis.

If Venus were to get so close to the Earth that it could actually exchange atmospheric contents as Velikovsky claimed . . . the Moon would have literally been flung into interplanetary space. At the very least its orbit would have been profoundly changed, made tremendously elliptical. . . . Had Venus done any of the things Velikovsky claimed, the Moon's orbit would have changed.[3]

Finally, in 1974, the American Association for the Advancement of Science invited Velikovsky himself to attend a meeting, where the scientific community completely dismissed his ideas. The absence of supporting material in ice core studies, bristlecone tree ring data, Swedish clay varves, and many hundreds of cores taken from ocean and lake sediments from all over the world, has ruled out any basis for Velikovsky's proposition of a global catastrophe within the Holocene age,[4] which represents the last 10,000 years of Earth's history, since the end of the ice age.

In his second book, *Ages in Chaos,* which was published in 1952, Velikovsky proposed to revise the chronology of the ancient Near East, claiming that the histories of Egypt and Israel are five centuries out of step.

The Scriptures tell of the sojourn of Israel in Egypt and of the Exodus; but no documents referring to these events have been found. . . . It is strange that there is no real link between the histories of Egypt and Palestine for a period of many hundreds of years. At least the Exodus of the Israelites from Egypt was an event that should belong to both historians and thus supply a connecting link. We shall therefore try to determine during what period of Egyptian history the Exodus took place. . . . The oldest theory places the Exodus at the earliest date: the Israelites were identified (by Josephus) with the Hyksos, and the Exodus was identified with the expulsion of the Hyksos. . . . Josephus Flavius, the Jewish historian of the first century, polemized against Apion, the grammarian, and against Manetho, his source, but accepted and supported the view that the Israelites were the Hyksos . . .

The identification of the Israelites with the Hyksos was many times accepted and as often rejected. Even today (in 1952) a group among the historians maintains that the Exodus took place at the very beginning of the Eighteenth Dynasty and that the story of the Exodus is but an echo of the expulsion of the Hyksos. However, in view of the bondage of the Israelites in Egypt and the bondage of Egypt under the Hyksos, the identity of martyred slaves and cruel tyrants must be regarded as a very strained hypothesis. . . . Apart from the incongruity of identifying the Hyksos with the Israelites, the tyrants with the oppressed, there is a further difficulty in the fact that during the time of the successors of Ahmose there was no likely moment for an invasion of Palestine by Israelite refugees from Egypt. The pharaohs who followed Ahmose were strong kings, and it is regarded as established that Palestine was under their domination.

The same argument was employed to defend the theory that the Exodus occurred in 1580, the time of the expulsion of the Hyksos: If the expulsion of the Hyksos (ca. 1580 BCE) is too early for the Exodus, where in the history of the powerful Eighteenth Dynasty can we find a probable place for an event, which, like the Exodus of tradition, presupposes internal trouble and weakness in Egypt, until the reign of Akhenaten?

In the 1880s, in the Nile Valley, at a place to which archaeologists gave the name of "Tell el-Amarna," a correspondence on clay tablets was found that dated from the time of Amenhotep III and his son Akhenaten. Some of them were anxious letters written from Jerusalem (Urusalim), warning the pharaoh of an invasion by the "Habiru (Khabiru)," approaching from Transjordan. Granting that the Habiru were identified with the Hebrews, the Exodus must

have taken place one or two generations earlier. . . . The end of
Akhenaten's reign and the close of the Eighteenth Dynasty in the
days of Tutankhamun and Aye was a time favorable for rebellion
and the withdrawal of the slaves from Egypt. No reference has been
found that could be interpreted as even hinting at an exodus during
the interregnum between the Eighteenth and Nineteenth Dynasties,
and only the fact that the situation was such as to make an exodus possible favors this hypothesis. [In fact the only historical evidence of an Exodus from Egypt to Canaan comes from the start
of the Nineteenth Dynasty as we shall see later.] This idea found
its way into the work of a psychologist who, following in the foot-
steps of certain historians [Strabo], tried to show that Moses was
an Egyptian prince, a pupil of Akhenaten; that Akhenaten was the
founder of monotheistic idealism; that when Akhenaten ceased to
rule and his schism fell into disfavor, Moses preserved his teachings
by bringing them to the slaves, with whom he left Egypt.[5]

Having dismissed all suggested dates for the Exodus, Velikovsky
introduces his own account by trying to explain Egyptian history
according to biblical events. He noted that the Bible refers to some
volcanic activity in the Sinai Peninsula at the time of the Exodus. For
after Pharaoh had given them permission to leave, the Israelites "took
their journey from Succoth. . . . And the Lord went before them by day
in a pillar of cloud to lead them the way; and by night in a pillar of
fire, to give them light; to go by day and by night" (Exodus 13:20-21).
Velikovsky explained:

The biblical story does not present the departure from Egypt as an
everyday occurrence, but rather as an event accompanied by violent
upheavals of nature. Grave and ominous signs preceded the Exodus:
clouds of dust and smoke darkened the sky and colored the water
they fell upon with a bloody hue. The dust tore wounds in the skin
of man and beast; in the torrid glow vermin and reptiles bred and
filled air and earth; wild beasts, plagued by sand and ashes, came
from the ravines of the wasteland to the bodies of men.[6]

The implications in the dating of Velikovsky's ancient biblical history were that the chronologies of ancient Egypt and ancient Israel were different by 500 years. It was his opinion that the Exodus was not in the era of Ramses II but occurred in the collapse of the Middle Kingdom of Egypt. The Hyksos, who invaded Egypt during the seventeenth century BCE, Velikovsky identified as being the same people as the biblical Amalekites. They were continuously attacking the fleeing Israelites, killing especially the women and children at the rear of the massive moving body of humans heading east away from Egypt.

Rather than agreeing with Josephus in identifying the Israelites with the Hyksos, or as he put it identifying "the Tyrants with the Oppressors," Velikovsky placed the Exodus not at the time of their invasion. His starting point in *Ages in Chaos* was that the Exodus took place, not as the orthodoxy has it, at some point during the Egyptian New Kingdom, but at the fall of the Middle Kingdom. Here he tried to use some biblical accounts of volcanic eruptions in Sinai to date the Israelites' Exodus, and argued that the history of Egypt is five centuries out of step. Thus Velikovsky's chronology places the Hyksos rule of Egypt shortly after the Israelite Exodus, and identified them as the biblical Amakites who fought the Israelites during their journey out of Egypt. Accordingly Velikovsky regarded Thutmose, who was mentioned by Manetho, as the Pharaoh of the Exodus.

Velikovsky's second step was to find some Egyptian evidence that can confirm the biblical account of volcanic eruptions in the country so as to link it to the Israelite Exodus. Here he found what he was looking for in a papyrus kept in the Leiden Museum in the Netherlands known as the "Ipuwer Papyrus," which, according to some Egyptologists, contains some prophecies and mentions a number of catastrophes that befell Egypt: "I came upon a reference to a sage, Ipuwer, who believed the fact that the river Nile had turned to blood. . . . I studied the text and came to the conclusion that I had a description of, not only a natural catastrophe, but precisely the plagues of Egypt."[7] As the biblical story reports that Egypt was punished by the Ten Plagues for Pharaoh's refusal to let the Israelites leave, he tried to find evidence of these plagues in order to fix the date of the Exodus. Velikovsky saw the Ipuwer account as evidence coming from an Egyptian scribe to the Ten Plagues reported by the Bible. Although the Bible does not relate these plagues to any volcanic activity, and mentions the pillars of smoke and fires only after the Israelites have left the border city of Succoth in their Exodus, Velikovsky claims that the Ten Plagues came as a result of volcanic eruption in Sinai.

The Ipuwer Papyrus was found in Egypt in the early nineteenth century, and was taken to the Leiden Museum and translated by Sir Alan Gardiner in 1909. The papyrus includes an ancient Egyptian poem, called "The Admonitions of Ipuwer," or the "Dialogue of Ipuwer, and the Lord of All." It was purchased by the Dutch Museum in 1828, from Giovanni Anastasi, the Swedish consul to Egypt, and has been dated to the later thirteenth century BCE, at the time of the Nineteenth Dynasty of Egypt. However, its text proved to be a copy of an earlier origin believed to be either the late Sixth Dynasty (ca. 1850 BCE) or the Second Intermediate Period (ca. 1600 BCE), and appears to describe how the Hyksos took over Egypt.

The Ipuwer Papyrus describes violent upheavals in Egypt: starvation, drought, escape of servants, breaking of prison, and death throughout the land. It describes Egypt as afflicted by natural disasters as a result of which it became in a state of chaos: the poor have become rich, and the rich have become poor, and warfare, famine, and death are everywhere. One symptom of this collapse of order is the lament that servants are leaving their servitude and acting rebelliously. However, Velikovsky, who saw this account as an Egyptian witness of Moses's Ten Plagues of Egypt, decided to revise the conventional chronology claiming that it came from the beginning of Egypt's Second Intermediate Period.

The starting point of this research was this: the Exodus from Egypt took place at the time of a great natural catastrophe. In order to find the time of the Exodus in Egyptian history, we had to search for some record of catastrophe in the physical world. This record is contained in the *Papyrus Ipuwer*. Many parts of the papyrus are missing. . . . But what is preserved is sufficient to impress us with this fact: before us is not merely the story of a catastrophe, but an Egyptian version of the plagues.[8]

In order to see if the Ipuwer Papyrus could really be related to the Ten Plagues of Moses we have to compare the papyrus text with the biblical story. Let us look at the Ten Plagues as they are found in the King James Version of the Bible, Book of Exodus.

1. Water to Blood: "And the Lord spake unto Moses, 'Say unto Aaron, Take thy rod, and stretch out thine hand upon the waters of Egypt, upon their streams, upon their rivers, and upon their ponds, and upon their pools of water, that they may become blood; and that there may be blood throughout all the land of Egypt, both in vessels of wood, and in vessels of stone.'" (7:19)

2. Frogs: "And if thou refuse to let them go, behold, I will smite thy borders with frogs. And the river shall bring forth frogs abundantly, which shall go up and come into thine house, and into thy bedchamber, and upon thy bed, and into the house of thy servants, and upon thy people, and into thine ovens, and into thy kneading troughs." (8:2–3)

3. Lice: "And the Lord said unto Moses, 'Say unto Aaron, stretch out thy rod, and smite the dust of the land that it may become lice throughout all the land of Egypt.'" (8:16)

4. Flies: "Else, if thou will not let my people go, behold, I will send swarms of flies upon thee, and upon thy servants, and upon thy people, and into thy houses: and the houses of the Egyptians shall be full of swarms of flies, and also the ground whereon they are." (8:21)

5. Livestock Diseased: "Behold, the hand of the Lord is upon thy cattle, which are in the field, upon the *horses,* upon the asses, upon the camels, upon the oxen, and upon the sheep: there shall be a very grievous murrain." (9:3)

6. Boils: "And the Lord said unto Moses and unto Aaron, 'Take to you handfuls of ashes of the furnace, and let Moses sprinkle it toward the heaven in the sight of Pharaoh. And it shall become small dust in all the land of Egypt, and shall be a boil breaking forth with blains upon man, and upon beast, throughout all the land of Egypt.'" (9:8–9)

7. Thunder and Hail: "Behold, tomorrow about this time I will cause it to rain a very grievous hail, such as hath not been in Egypt since the foundation thereof until now." (9:18)

8. Locusts: "Else, if thou refuse to let my people go, behold, tomorrow will I bring the locusts into thy coast: and they shall cover the face of the earth, that one cannot be able to see the earth: and they shall eat the residue of that which is escaped, which remaineth unto you from the hail, and shall eat every tree which groweth for you out of the field." (10:4–5)

9. Darkness: "And the Lord said unto Moses, 'Stretch out thine hand toward heaven, that there may be darkness over the land of Egypt, even darkness which may be felt.' And Moses stretched forth his hand toward heave; and there was a thick darkness in all the land of Egypt for three days." (10:21–22)

10. Death of the Firstborn: "And Moses said, 'Thus saith the Lord, About midnight will I go out into the midst of Egypt: And all the firstborn in the land shall die, from the firstborn of Pharaoh that sitteth upon his throne, even unto the firstborn of the maidservant that is behind the mill; and all the firstborn of beasts.'" (11:4–5)

Except for the death of the firstborn, all the other plagues are common natural events that still occur every year even until this day in Egypt. Until the building of the High Dam in 1970, the water of the Nile turned red every year between June and September, as a result of the annual flood with its rich alluvial deposits coming from the Ethiopian volcanic mountains. As for flies, lice, and locusts, these were also common thing in ancient Egypt:

Many insects tormented the ancient Egyptians; flies, lice, fleas, bedbugs, and worst of all, mosquitoes and locusts. . . . There was little one could do about such a plague, such as the fertility god Min, protector of crops, or Isis as guardian of life. Their livelihood was also threatened by weevils and grain beetles which destroyed stored grain.[9]

Locusts still attack Egypt until the present time, as can be shown by the BBC report on November 18, 2004.

Swarms of locusts blown off the Mediterranean towards the Egyptian capital, Cairo.

. . . Millions of the insects swept into Cairo and the surrounding Nile Delta region throughout Wednesday. The infestation of the red desert locusts was Egypt's largest since the 1950s. UN officials believe the locusts, which can consume vast swathes of crops in warm weather, will head to the sea.[10]

As for the darkness that covered Egypt for three days in the time of Moses, it is still happening yearly until the present time as a result of wind known as Khamasin, "dust storms," which comes from the western desert and lasts fifty days, during March and April, when the sky becomes yellow.

When we compare this with the text of the Ipuwer Papyrus we do find agreement on few points only, such as the water turning to blood: "the river is blood and one drinks from it" (2:10); livestock troubles: "Behold, cattle are left to stray, and there is none to gather them together" (9:2–3); although the mention of *horses* among livestock indicates a date after the Hyksos rule, as Egypt had no horses before their arrival. Darkness is also mentioned by Ipuwer: "The land is without light" (9:11).

On the other hand, the Egyptian scribe has no mention of frogs, lice, flies, boils, thunder, and hail, and above all, Ipuwer has no mention of the most important of the biblical plagues: the killing of the firstborn in all the land, including Pharaoh's own son. Throughout the history of ancient Egypt, the annual flooding of the Nile to inundate the fields on its valley was relied upon to feed the population. The collapse of the Old Kingdom pyramid builders was due to low flood levels, which resulted in famine that came as a result of low levels of the Nile inundation that lasted for many years. This situation caused chaos and disorder that led to the fall of the central government and the spread of vandalism. The Ipuwer Papyrus describes this kind of situation:

"Lower Egypt weeps. The entire palace is without its revenues. To it belong wheat and barley, geese and fish" (10:3–6). And again "grain has perished on every side" (6:3), "the children of princes are dashed against the wall" (4:3), and "the children of princes are cast out in the streets" (6:12). "The prison is ruined" (6:3). "He who places his brother in the ground is everywhere" (2:13), and "Gold and lapis lazuli, silver and malachite, carnelian and bronze . . . are fastened on the neck of female slaves" (3:2).

Velikovsky wrote a number of books, in all of which he attempted to validate the chronology of the Hebrew Bible by proving the historicity of miracles and myth, against historical and archaeological evidence.

When I began my search about Moses and the Israelite Exodus, about the same time that Velikovsky died in 1979, I decided to follow the opposite road. Rather than trying to fit historical events into the unproven biblical chronology, I tried to fit biblical events into Egyptian chronology.

8

THE MIRACLE OF SANTORINI

The Exodus story, with its miraculous events, has fascinated people of all different faiths for more than 2,000 years. Using his magical rod, Moses was able to punish Egypt and its Pharaoh with the Ten Plagues, and divided the waters of the Red Sea; allowing the Israelites to cross to Sinai while Pharaoh and his soldiers were drowned in the surging waves. In modern times, however, people felt the need to have a scientific explanation of these miraculous events. Not long after the 1979 death of Velikovsky, whose comet theories had failed to satisfy the scientific community, another catastrophic theory appeared. This time the miraculous events of the Exodus were explained, not as a result of a change in Earth orbit, but as a result of a volcanic eruption that caused massive destruction in the mid-second millennium BCE. In December 28, 1985, the *New York Times* published the story.

Probing 20 feet into the soil of the Nile Delta, American scientists have found tiny glass fragments from a volcano that they say could lend support to a theory linking a volcanic eruption with the seemingly miraculous events associated with the Exodus of the Israelites from Egypt. Scholars for some time have tied the devastating eruption 3,500 years ago in Santorini, a Greek island also known as Thera, with legends of the lost continent of Atlantis and have cited it as a major factor in the fall of the Minoan civilization on Crete.

More recently the eruption has been invoked to explain phenomena related to the Exodus, as described in the Bible. According to this controversial theory, the ash cloud from the eruption could account for the "deep darkness over the whole land of Egypt, even a darkness that may be felt," and the ensuing tidal wave could have created the "parting of the waves" that swallowed the pursuing Egyptians and allowed the Israelites to escape.

Santorini, classically and officially Thera, is an island in the southern Aegean Sea, about 200 km (120 miles) southeast from Greece's mainland. It is the largest island of a small, circular archipelago, which bears the same name and is the remnant of a volcanic caldera. It forms the southernmost member of the Cyclades group of islands, with an area of approximately 73 sq km (28 sq miles) and a 2001 census population of 13,670. The Minoan eruption of Santorini, also referred to as the Thera eruption,

Fig. 8.1. Santorini Volcano.

was a major catastrophic volcanic eruption with a Volcanic Explosivity Index (VEI) of 6 or 7 and a Dense Rock Equivalent (DRE) of 60 km. Its eruption was one of the largest volcanic events on Earth in recorded history, which devastated the Island of Santorini, including the Minoan settlement at Akrotiri, as well as communities and agricultural areas on nearby islands and on the coast of Crete. This major eruption resulted in an ash plume estimated at 30 to 35 km (19 to 22 miles) high, which extended into the stratosphere. In addition, the magma underlying the volcano came into contact with the shallow marine embayment, resulting in a volcanic steam eruption. The eruption also generated a tsunami 35 to 150 m (115 to 490 feet) high that devastated the north coast of Crete, 110 km (68 miles) to the south. Ash layers in cores drilled from the seabed and from lakes in Turkey, however, show that the heaviest ash fall was toward the east and northeast of Santorini.

Although the Santorini eruption provides a fixed point for chronology in the Aegean settlements, as evidence of the eruption was found throughout the region, there has been some disagreement on the date of the eruption itself. While archaeological evidence dates the eruption during the founding on the New Kingdom in Egypt around 1500 BCE, radiocarbon and tree-ring dating placed the eruption more than a century earlier, between 1635 and 1616 BCE. The tsunami created by the Santorini eruption is believed to have led to the collapse of the Minoan civilization on the island of Crete.

The Minoan civilization, the first Greek civilization in history, appeared during the Bronze Age on the island of Crete. It flourished as a maritime power from approximately the twenty-seventh century to the fifteenth century BCE, and was able to dominate the shores and islands of the Aegean Sea. Nevertheless, all of a sudden, at the height of its power, the Minoan civilization was mysteriously destroyed, leaving important tokens of its grandeur. Unknown in modern times, the Minoan civilization was only rediscovered at the beginning of the twentieth century by the British archaeologist Arthur Evans who, in the 1900s, excavated and restored the ruins at Knossos, at the site of Heraklion. Beautiful and delicate frescoes of bulls and dolphins revealed a highly artistic civilization and a people who apparently lived in harmony with nature. The excavated Minoan palace at Knossos was found to be a vast and elaborate structure, with Europe's first paved roads and running water. It became clear that the eruption on the island of Santorini, about 68 miles from Crete, devastated the nearby Minoan settlement at Akrotiri on Santorini, which was entombed in a layer of pumice. Fifty years after the Santorini eruption, Minoan civilization completely disappeared. While no ancient records of the eruption have been found, the eruption seems to have inspired some Greek myths, as the ancient Greeks wove Minoan magnificence into their myths; it was the home of King Minos and his man-eating bull, the Minotaur, who roamed the palace labyrinth.

The first speculators in modern times associated Minoan Crete with the lost continent of Atlantis that was referred to in the works of Plato, the Greek philosopher. In his dialogues *Timaeus* and *Critias,* written about 360 BCE, Plato first mentioned the legendary island of Atlantis, a naval power lying "in front of the Pillars of Hercules," which in antiquity was the name of the Strait of Gibraltar between the Mediterranean and the Atlantic Ocean. Atlantis, he wrote, conquered many parts of Western Europe and Africa 9,000 years before the time of Solon, the Athenian lawmaker who lived during the sixth century BCE. After a failed attempt to invade Athens, the story goes, Atlantis sank into the ocean "in a single day and night of misfortune." Some scholars argue Plato drew upon memories of past events such as the Santorini eruption or the Trojan War; nevertheless, the possible existence of a genuine Atlantis was generally rejected. Alan Cameron states: "It is only in modern times that people have taken the Atlantis story seriously, no one did so in antiquity."[1]

However, following the general rejection of Velikovsky's theories by the academic community, a number of people have attempted to connect the volcanic eruption in Santorini to the Ten Plagues of Moses, as well as the parting of the Red Sea. For instance, Hans Goedicke, professor emeritus of Near Eastern Studies at John Hopkins University in Maryland, and the British popular author Ian Wilson claim that the crossing of the Red Sea was made possible by a huge tidal wave that resulted from the eruption of the volcano Santorini. Professor Costas Synolakis, a tsunami expert, also believes that the massive volcanic eruption on the island of Santorini, which he dates in 1600 BCE, could have generated a giant tidal wave that struck the Nile Delta. This incredibly powerful wave, he thinks, could be linked to the story of the Red Sea parting into walls of water that was written centuries later. Like Velikovsky's theories before, these new arguments soon became popular, especially when they were presented on television. On Easter Day, April 16, 2006, a ninety-minute documentary program was aired on The Discovery Channel Canada, and shown on August 20 of the same year in the United States on the History Channel. The documentary, created by Israeli-Canadian filmmaker Simcha Jacobovici, and produced by James Cameron, claimed that the Exodus took place around 1500 BCE, during the reign of Ahmose I, which according to the program coincided with the Minoan eruption. The program explained Moses's Ten Plagues that ravaged Egypt as being the result of that eruption. Jacobovici, following Josephus, suggested that the Hyksos were the same people as the Hebrews of the Bible, and claimed that the mention of a "great storm" in a stele of Ahmose I refers to Moses's plagues, presenting the death of Ahmose's son, Ahmose Sapair, at the age of twelve, as a confirmation of the biblical account of the death of Pharaoh's firstborn.

This argument was strengthened when Egyptian archaeologists announced that they have found traces of solidified Santorini lava on the northern coast of Sinai, which they dated to around 1500 BCE. On April 2, 2007, Zahi Hawass, who was then Secretary General of the Supreme Council for Antiquities (SCA), told National Geographic News that the lava and ash came "from Santorini, an eastern Mediterranean volcano that had been linked to the myth of Atlantis."[2] Hawass hailed the discovery as opening a "new field" of study in Egyptology, hoping that "Geologists will help us study how natural disasters, such as the Santorini tsunami, affected the pharaonic period."[3]

Egyptian archaeologists also theorized that the Santorini volcano created a tsunami that swept the lava all the way to Egypt. They showed white stones of pumice, which they believed the tsunami carried 850 km (528 miles) across the Mediterranean to north Sinai. This find seemed to show that Santorini produced a tremendously powerful blast, and the ash cloud covered a wide area including Egypt. It also added some spark to a long-standing debate among archaeologists and historians over the date of the Exodus, for which the Bible notes: "for three days there was deep darkness over the whole land of Egypt" (Exodus 10:21). However, some experts doubted that the lava from the volcano could have reached Sinai that way and suggested the deposits found in Egypt were carried in later time by regular currents. Georges Vougioukalakis, a volcanologist at Greece's Institute of Geology and Mineral Exploration, was skeptical that the pumice could have traveled so far. "Thin strata of ash—carried by the wind from Santorini—have already been found in the Nile Delta, the tsunami could have carried pumice a bit higher than the coastal area. But it would have been carried there by currents."[4]

At the same time, as some people are trying to date the Exodus according to the Santorini eruption, scholars are still divided on the exact date of this eruption itself. While tree-ring dating indicates a massive volcanic eruption in 1628 BCE, archaeologists have dated the eruption to 1500 BCE based on the style of pottery that was destroyed in the Santorini eruption. Professor Colin Humphreys, the British physicist and Director of Research at Cambridge University, offered another reason for rejecting the volcanic theory.

The suggestion that the Red Sea crossing was made possible by a tsunami caused by an underwater volcanic eruption in the Red Sea, which sent huge tidal waves up the Gulfs of Aqaba and Suez, does not fit the Exodus account itself. A tsunami would cause rapid flooding followed by rapid recession of the water. The whole point of the Exodus account is that these events happened the other way round: first the water receded, enabling the Israelites to cross, and then it returned, drowning the Egyptian army. So we can rule out tsunami, due to Santorini or any other volcano, as the mechanism for the Red Sea crossing.[5]

While people now living in the modern scientific age do feel the need to have physical evidence to confirm the story of Moses and the Exodus, the attempt to prove their historicity by trying to confirm biblical miracles scientifically is not the right way to do it. What modern people really need is historical confirmation of Moses himself and his Exodus. Miracles are matters of belief and theology, which has nothing to do with history and science. In science, events are explained naturalistically, by appealing to laws of nature, while miracles could not be explained scientifically. They are events attributed to divine intervention, which represent an interruption of the laws of nature. No scientific evidence could ever be found to prove that Moses was able to divide the waters of the sea, and make it stand in two separate walls. In this case, it would be better to abandon this fruitless attempt of confirming biblical miraculous events, and concentrate on the story of Moses and the Israelites themselves.

9

JOSEPH'S MUMMY IN THE CAIRO MUSEUM

My own involvement in the search for the Israelite Exodus had a different reason and a different route. As an Egyptian, I was a devout Muslim who said his prayers five times a day and read the Qu'ran early every morning. In 1947, the year that marked the outbreak of the first hostilities between Egypt and the Jews in Palestine, I was only thirteen. At the elementary school, I was taught religion by Hassan al-Banna, who in 1928 had established the Muslim Brotherhood. This was the first movement of political Islam in modern times; its main aim was to reestablish the Islamic caliphate, dissolved by Kemal Ataturk in Turkey in 1924. I was persuaded eventually to join the Brotherhood, which I believed would establish the rule of God on Earth. While British Mandate over Palestine was approaching its end, the Brotherhood decided to form a Fidaeyin military unit to go and fight the Haganah and the Irgun, the two Jewish military organizations in Palestine. As this was a holy war, I was quite happy to fight and, if necessary, die for the victory of my God. I decided to join the military unit confident that I had nothing to lose; if I manage to defeat the Jews, I would have defeated the enemies of God, and if I were to die, I would become a martyr and go to heaven straight away, without even going through the hall of judgment. My wish was not fulfilled, however—as I was underage, I was not allowed to fight.

By the time another round of hostilities threatened, in the early 1960s, my views had changed markedly. In the intervening years I had studied law and found myself a job as a journalist. I had also become absorbed in the apparently irrational enmity that existed between Egypt and Israel. Why could they not agree to live peacefully together? Why would they not settle their differences by talking instead of fighting? The hostility between the two peoples struck me as being like a bitter, long-running family feud, whose roots must lie buried in the deep past of our forgotten common history. Instead of joining the war, this time I wanted to uncover the roots of the Israeli-Egyptian conflict. After all it was in Egypt that the Israelites arrived as a minor Hebrew tribe, and left as an important nation. Moses, the great Lawgiver of the Jews, was born in Egypt, brought up in the royal palace, and received the Torah on Mount Sinai. Unable to find historical information about the ancient Israelites in my country, I decided to leave Cairo for London in December 1964. However, to my disappointment, I soon found out that even in the British capital, no single biblical character had been identified from Egyptian sources, and no agreement had been reached between scholars on the time of the Exodus. It was then that I realized that the road ahead of me was to be a long one.

I enrolled in an evening course to study the history of ancient Egypt for three years, run by the Egypt Exploration Society and London University, then spent another three years studying hieroglyphics. I also taught myself classical Hebrew, which, like Arabic, is a Semitic language. To start my search, I then joined the British Library, which at the time was still located inside the British Museum. Although now I was able to delve deeply into ancient sources and follow-up reports of modern archaeology, it was to be a familiar biblical text that gave me the first break. One winter's night in 1985, I awakened just after midnight and found I could not go back to sleep. I made myself a cup of tea and sat by the fire, reading again—as I often did—the story of Joseph in the Old Testament. On this occasion, however, I was struck suddenly by a passage in the Book of Genesis that I had passed over many times before without attaching any particular significance to it. It occurs when, at a time of famine, Joseph's half-brothers make the second of the two visits to Egypt to buy corn. Joseph recognized Jacob's sons when he saw them, but they did not recognize him in his Egyptian costume as he spoke harshly to them through an interpreter.

Joseph invited them to have a meal in his house and then, in an emotional moment, he revealed his identity to his brothers. They were ashamed of what they had done to him when they sold him as a slave, but he asked them not to feel any sense of guilt: "For God did send me before you to preserve life, and He has made me a *father to Pharaoh,*" he said.

Father to Pharaoh! It was then, in the middle of the night, that I realized that this was an Egyptian title. Egyptian officials were usually given the title "Son of Pharaoh," but "Father to Pharaoh" was a rare title and only one person is known to have received it in the New Kingdom. Immediately the name of Yuya came to my mind. Yuya served as a minister and commander of the military chariots for Amenhotep III (ca. 1405 BCE–1367 BCE) of the Eighteenth Dynasty. Among his many titles, Yuya bore one that was unique to him, *it ntr n nb tawi,* the "holy father of the Lord of the Two Lands," Pharaoh's formal title, inscribed on the *ushabit* (meaning "funeral statuette") in his tomb, and more than twenty times on his funerary papyrus. The reason for Yuya to get this rare and unique title was the fact that the king, Amenhotep III, in his Year 2, married Yuya's daughter, Tiye, and made her his queen against Egyptian traditions, which allows only the heiress, the king's sister, to become the queen. Amenhotep III issued a special scarab to announce this marriage: "Live . . . King Amenhotep (III), who is given life, (and) the Great King's Wife Tiye, who liveth. The name of her father is Yuya, the name of her mother is Tuya. She is the wife of a mighty king whose southern boundary is as far as Karoy (in northern Sudan) and the northern as far as Naharin (in northern Syria)."[1]

Fig. 9.1. Amenhotep II and Queen [Yite] Tiye at the Cairo Museum.
Photo courtesy of Ahmed Osman.

COULD JOSEPH THE PATRIARCH AND YUYA BE THE SAME PERSON?

It seemed to me like a flash of inspiration, an unexpected moment of revelation when I couldn't sleep that night, waiting for the library to open at ten o'clock in the morning to go and check the details of Yuya's life. I felt that I was about to resolve a problem to which many gifted scholars had devoted their minds without success for more than a century: identifying a major biblical figure as the same person as a major Egyptian historical figure. Since the start of archaeological digging in Egypt, about a century and a half ago, scholars have been trying to answer this question: During which period did Joseph live, and who was the king who appointed him as his minister? Now, if Yuya and Joseph could be identified as being the same person, the time of the Israelite arrival in Egypt could be easily fixed.

JOSEPH

The biblical story of Joseph begins in chapter 37 of the Book of Genesis, when he is seventeen years old, and occupies virtually all the remainder of this book. Jacob, we are told, loved Joseph more than he loved any of his other sons and made him a richly ornamented robe with many colors. His half-brothers envied Joseph because of this favoritism, and they hated him even more when he related to them a dream he had had. "We were binding sheaves of corn in the field when suddenly my sheaf rose and stood upright, while your sheaves gathered round mine and bowed to it," he explained. "Do not think one day you will be lord over us?" the angry brothers asked. Then Joseph had a second dream, which he related to his father as well as his brothers: "The sun, the moon, and eleven stars bowed down to me." It served to fuel the brothers' jealousy, and Jacob rebuked Joseph, saying: "What is this dream of yours? Must your mother and I and your brothers come and bow down to the ground before you?"

One day, Joseph was at home with his father while the brothers were supposedly grazing their sheep near Shecham, an ancient Canaanite city near Nablus on the West Bank. Jacob said to him: "Go and see if all is well with your brothers and with the sheep, and bring word back to me." Joseph set off, but on arriving at Shecham could find neither his brothers nor their sheep, as they had gone to Dothan about 100 km (62 miles) north of Hebron. Joseph went after them and, when they saw him approaching in the distance, the brothers said to each other: "Here comes the dreamer. Let's kill him and throw him into one of these pits and say that a wild animal devoured him. Then we'll see what comes of his dreams." Finally, however, they decided to sell him as a slave to a caravan of Ishmaelite traders who were on their way down to Egypt, for twenty shekels of silver.

In Egypt, the Ishmaelites sold Joseph to Potiphar, one of Pharaoh's officials, the captain of the guard. When Potiphar found the young man to be a faithful servant, he entrusted to Joseph's care his entire household. But Joseph was not only efficient, he was also a handsome young man, and soon Potiphar's wife took notice of him and wanted him to lie with her. When Joseph rejected her invitation, she accused him of attempting to rape her. As a result Joseph was sent to prison where he met two prisoners who had dreams that he interpreted for them, and his interpretation proved to be fulfilled. Three days later, on Pharaoh's birthday, Pharaoh's baker was executed, and his cupbearer was released to be restored to his job. Before the cupbearer's release, Joseph asked the cupbearer to speak to Pharaoh about him, but he forgot until, two years later, when Pharaoh himself had two mysterious dreams. It was then that the cupbearer told Pharaoh of Joseph's power to interpret dreams, and Pharaoh ordered for Joseph to be brought from prison instantly.

Pharaoh explained to Joseph: "In my dream I was standing on the bank of the Nile when out of the river there came seven cows, fat and sleek, and they grazed among the reeds." He went on, "After them appeared seven other cows: scrawny and very gaunt and lean. These lean, gaunt cows ate up the seven fat ones. But even after they ate them no one could tell that they had done so; they looked as gaunt as before.

"In my dreams I also saw seven ears of corn, full and good, growing on a single stalk. After them, seven other ears sprouted: withered and thin and blighted by the east wind. The thin ears swallowed up the seven good ears. I told this to the magicians, but none could explain it to me."

In his interpretation, Joseph told Pharaoh that Egypt will have seven years of plenty, but they will be followed by seven years of famine. Then all the abundance in Egypt will be forgotten, and the famine will ravage the land. He advised Pharaoh to look for a shrewd and wise man and put him in charge of the country. "Let Pharaoh appoint commissioners to take a fifth of the harvest of Egypt during the seven years of abundance. They should store up the grain under the authority of Pharaoh, to be kept in the cities for food." Impressed by what he heard, Pharaoh said to Joseph: "There is no one so shrewd and wise as you. You shall be in charge of my household, and all my people are to submit to your orders. Only in respect of the throne shall I be greater than you."

At the celebration of his appointment to his new job, Pharaoh took his signet ring from his own hand and placed it on Joseph's finger. He gave him a chariot and dressed him in robes of fine linen, put a gold chain around his neck, and arranged for Joseph to ride in a chariot as his second-in-command. In addition, the king gave him an Egyptian name, starting with "Zaph" or "Seph," as well as an Egyptian wife, Asenath, daughter of the priest of On (Heliopolis).

Joseph, who was thirty years old at the time, became a father of two sons, Manasseh and Ephraim during the seven good years. Then came the predicted years of famine, which affected Egypt as well as Canaan, where Jacob said to his sons: "I have heard that there is corn in Egypt. Go down there and buy some so that we don't starve." The brothers set off, leaving behind their younger brother, Benjamin, Joseph's only full brother. In Egypt, Joseph accused his brothers of being spies, and pretended that he did not believe their accounts of innocence. He insisted that they should leave one of them as a hostage until they came back with their youngest brother, Benjamin. Although Jacob refused to let Benjamin go, as the famine was sore in Canaan, he eventually agreed that the brothers could take him and return to buy corn in Egypt. This time, Joseph invited them to have a meal in his house. Although he had hatched a plot designed to ensure that Benjamin would have to stay in Egypt, accusing him of stealing his silver cup, in an emotional moment Joseph decided to reveal himself to his brothers. "Come close to me," he said, and when they had approached him went on,

> I am your brother Joseph, the one you sold into Egypt. And now, do not be distressed and do not be angry with yourselves for selling me here, because it was God who sent me ahead of you to save lives. . . . So it was not you who sent me here, but God. He has made me a father to Pharaoh, lord over all his household and ruler of all Egypt. Now hurry back to my father and tell him.

When Pharaoh heard that Joseph's brothers were in Egypt, he said to him: "Tell your brothers: Load your animals and go back to Canaan, and bring your father and your families back to me. I shall give you the best land in Egypt" (Genesis 45:17). When his family arrived, Joseph drove his chariot out to meet them, and, after an emotional reunion, Jacob said to him: "Now I am ready to die, since I have seen for myself that you are still alive." Joseph then settled all his family in the land of Goshen at the Sinai border, and introduced his father and five of his brothers to Pharaoh.

Seventeen years later, Jacob, who felt that the time of his death was approaching, sent for Joseph and said to him: "Do not bury me in Egypt, but when I die carry me out of Egypt and bury me where my forefathers are buried." Later, when Jacob eventually died, Joseph gave orders for him to be embalmed and, after seventy days of mourning, asked permission to take his father's body back to Canaan for burial. Pharaoh granted his request. It was an impressive caravan that set out for Canaan with all the adults from Joseph's and his brothers' families, all the dignitaries of Egypt, as well as Egyptian chariots and horsemen. A short time after his father's death, we come to the account of Joseph's own death. No indication is given of how much time had elapsed since the death of Jacob, but we are told that Joseph saw the third generation of Ephraim's children, indicating that he died at an old age. The Book of Genesis ends with Joseph's death and his burial according to

Egyptian customs: "So Joseph died at the age of a hundred and ten. And after they embalmed him he was laid in a coffin in Egypt."

YUYA

The tomb of Yuya and his wife Tuya was found in 1905, three years after the American Theodore M. Davis had obtained a concession to excavate in the Valley of the Kings. Davis provided the money, while the actual work was carried out by British archaeologists. The site of the tomb, the only one in Egypt to be found almost intact until the discovery of Tutankhamun's seventeen years later, occasioned some surprise. There is a narrow side valley in the Valley of the Kings, about half a mile long, leading up to the mountain. Eight days before Christmas of 1904, James Quibell started the examination of this side valley. A month later, he decided to transfer the men back to the mouth of the side valley, and by February 1 they had exposed the top of a sealed door that blocked the stairwell. In few days' time Davis and his group were able to enter the tomb, in which they found the sarcophagus of Yuya and of his wife, Tuya, including their mummies. Although both Yuya and his wife were known from other historical sources, neither was considered particularly important to be buried in the Valley of the Kings. From the objects in the tomb, it became clear that Yuya was an important official in Pharaoh's government, being so close to the king who entrusted him with many important duties. When Yuya's mummy was lifted out of his coffin, a necklace of large beads, made of gold and lapis lazuli and strung on a strong thread, was found behind his mummy's neck. His mummy was so well preserved that it seemed to Arthur Weigall, one of the archaeologists involved in the discovery, as if he might open his eyes and talk. Among his many titles we find:

> Master of the Horse
> Deputy of His Majesty in the Chariotry
> Bearer of the Ring of the King of Lower Egypt
> Seal-bearer of the King of Lower Egypt
> Hereditary Noble and Count

Overseer of the Cattle of Min, Lord of Akhmim
Confidant of the King
First of the Friends
The Wise One

Yuya's wife, Tuya, occupied an important position in the Royal Palace. She was the "king's ornament," a post that might be said to combine the duties of a modern butler and lady-in-waiting, which would require her to live in the royal residence. In these circumstances we can understand how young King Amenhotep III grew up with Tuya's daughter, Tiye, became enchanted with her, and married her. Unlike Tuya his wife, who had conventional Egyptian looks, Yuya has remarkably foreign appearance. Arthur Weigall, a British Egyptologist of the early twentieth century, made the point in 1910 in his book *The Life and Times of Akhenaten:* "He [Yuya] was a person of commanding presence, whose powerful character showed itself in his face. One must picture him now as a tall man with a fine shock of white hair; a great hooked nose like that of a Syrian; full, strong lips; and a prominent, determined jaw. He has the face of an ecclesiastic, and there is something about his mouth that reminds one of the late Pope Leo III."

Henri Naville, the Swiss archaeologist, remarked that Yuya's very aquiline face might be Semitic, while Grafton Eliot Smith, the British anatomist who examined Yuya's mummy in 1905, raised the question of his non-Egyptian appearance. Commenting on Yuya's appearance and his origin, he noticed that "his nose is prominent, aquiline, and high-bridged." On the subject of Yuya's origin, Smith observed that his mummy "has a distinctively alien appearance."

There are other indications that Yuya was of foreign origin. His name, which was not known in Egypt before him, proved difficult to render into hieroglyphics. Eleven different versions of Yuya's name were found in his tomb, on his sarcophagus, the three coffins, and other funerary furniture: *Ya, Yaa, Yiya, Yuya, Yayai, Yu, Yuyu, Yaya, Yiay, Yia,* and *Yuy,* which makes one wonder what was the name the craftsmen were trying to inscribe? Egyptian names usually included the name of the deity under whose protection the person was placed: Ra-mose,

Fig. 9.2. Queen Tiye's head, from my book Moses and Akhenaten.

Ptah-mose, Amun-hotep, and so on. The evidence suggests that, despite the years he spent in Egypt and the high office he held, Joseph remained aloof from Egyptian religious worship. It seems, therefore, a reasonable assumption that by the time Joseph died, Egyptians must have realized that he would not accept the protection of any other gods, only that of his own Yhwh or Yhwe (Jehovah), and what they were trying to write, following their traditions, was the name of this God. The two parts of Yuya's name, *Yu* and *Ya* are both short for the name of Yhwe, the Hebrew letter Y (J in English) being in both parts. For instant, Yu is the first part of the Hebrew Yuhana, "John" in English, as Ya is the first part of the Hebrew Yashu, "Joshua" in English.

Joseph's name seems to have been combined of two elements, the Hebrew Yu and the Egyptian Seph. This is confirmed by the fact that, according to the Bible, Pharaoh gave him an Egyptian name starting with Zaph or Seph. At the same time, Manetho, when talking about Moses, speaks of Osar-Seph, as the leader of the religious rebellion at the time of Amenhotep III and Yuya.

It is noticeable that two of the three objects that were given to Joseph by Pharaoh when he appointed him in his service, the golden chain and the chariot, were found in Yuya's tomb. At the same time, although the royal ring was not found in his tomb, written evidence was found to show that Yuya was bearer of the king's ring. This is clear from two of Yuya's titles, "Bearer of the Seal of the King of Lower Egypt" as well as "Bearer of the Ring of the King of Lower Egypt." Both Yuya and Joseph lived to an old age, for although the average age at the time did not exceed thirty-five years, Yuya, according to the estimation of Grafton Elliot Smith, was not less than sixty at the time of his death, and Henri Naville, who translated Yuya's Book of the Dead, noted that the artist gave him a white wig to indicate his old age. In the case of Joseph, although we can't take seriously the age of one hundred and ten years given by the Bible, he is reported to have seen his great-grandchildren before he died.

Nevertheless, one essential point was still missing to confirm that Yuya and Joseph were the same person. For although both characters are known to have had two sons—Yuya had Anen and Aye, while Joseph had Manasseh and Ephraim—there is no mention in the Bible that Joseph had a daughter, while it is well known that Yuya had a daughter, Queen Tiye. However, when we examine the biblical account carefully, we find a strong indication that Joseph also had a daughter. For while the Bible states that all the family of Jacob who went to Egypt, including Joseph and his children, were numbered seventy persons, the total names it gives comes only to sixty-nine, and number seventy remains unnamed, which most probably was Joseph's daughter. What strengthens this conclusion is the fact that, when Jacob died and Joseph wanted to bury him in Canaan, he did not go to Pharaoh for permission, but "spake to *the house* of Pharaoh, saying, 'If now I have found grace in your eyes, speak, I pray you, in the ears of Pharaoh'" (Genesis 50:4). In Egypt, until this day, "the house of a man" is an expression that means "his wife." Why should Joseph speak to the queen instead of going directly to the king unless she was nearer to him than the king?

THE TIME OF JOSEPH

Although modern scholars no longer accepted Josephus's identification of the Israelites with the Hyksos they, nevertheless, regarded the early part of the Hyksos rule as the right time for Joseph's arrival in Egypt. Eric Peet, the British Egyptologist of the early twentieth century, explained in his *Egypt and the Old Testament:*

> Such is the period in which the entry of the Hebrews into Egypt would seem most naturally to fall. It would explain very simply the fact that the newcomers at first met with good treatment at the hands of the King of Egypt, for from the point of view of a people dwelling in Goshen, probably a region in the eastern delta, the King of Egypt would be the Hyksos reigning at Avaris, doubtless related by race to the Hebrews themselves, and not the Egyptian king reigning, probably in a half-dependent state, at Thebes in Upper Egypt.[2]

This view, however, contradicts the Bible story itself where the narrator refers to the Hebrew shepherds, on two occasions, as being

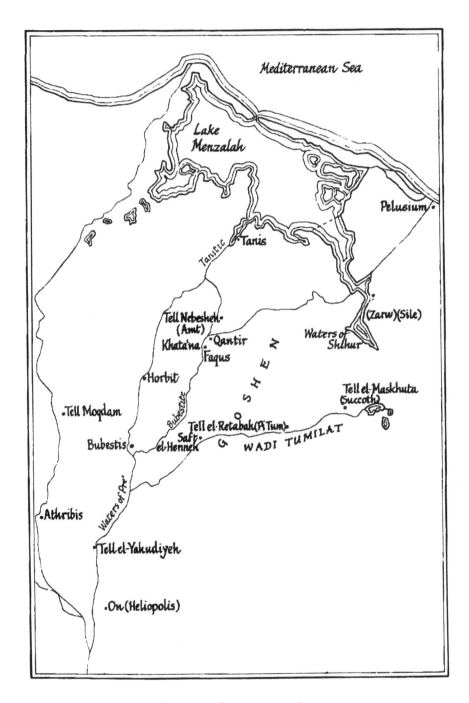

Fig. 9.3. The Eastern Delta.

an abomination to Egyptians. The first mention occurs when Joseph invited his brothers to have a meal in his home: "And they [Joseph's attendants] set on for him by himself and for them by themselves and for the Egyptians, which did eat with him, by themselves: because the Egyptians might not eat bread with the Hebrews; for that is an abomination unto the Egyptians" (Genesis 43:32). The second mention occurs after Jacob and his Israelite family have arrived in Egypt to settle and Joseph's brothers are about to have an audience with Pharaoh. Joseph warns them: "And it shall come to pass, when Pharaoh shall call you, and shall say, 'What is your occupation?' that ye shall say, 'Thy servants' trade hath been about cattle from our youth even until now, both we, and also our fathers: that ye may dwell in the land of Goshen; for every shepherd is an abomination unto the Egyptians'" (Genesis 46:33–34). If Joseph's Hebrew family had arrived in Egypt during the Hyksos rule, however, it would be difficult to imagine that a Hyksos king, himself a ruler of shepherds, would consider Joseph's family an abomination on account of their being shepherds. The Egyptian evidence shows that it was during the Eighteenth Dynasty, after the expulsion of the Hyksos, that the Asiatic shepherds became particularly distrusted. Only in recent years has it become clear that from the time of the New Kingdom onward, beginning after the expulsion of the Hyksos, the Egyptians tightened their control over the flow of immigrants from Canaan into the *delta*. They established a system of forts along the delta's eastern border and manned them with garrison troops and administrators. A late-thirteenth-century papyrus records how closely the commanders of the forts monitored the movements of foreigners.

We have completed the entry of the tribes of the Edomite Shasu [i.e., Bedouin] through the fortress of Menepta-Content-with-Truth, which is in *Tlkw,* to the pools of *Pr-Itm,* which [are] in *Tjkw* for the sustenance of their flocks. . . . The border between Canaan and Egypt was thus closely controlled.[3]

CHARIOTS

Up to the last decades of the twentieth century there was another reason for Egyptologists to prefer the Hyksos period for the arrival of Joseph in Egypt. They noticed that "chariots" were mentioned three times in Joseph's story.

1. When Pharaoh appointed Joseph as his minister, he gave Joseph a chariot.
2. When Jacob arrived in Egypt, Joseph used a chariot to go and welcome his father.
3. When Joseph went to bury his father in Canaan, he took with him "both chariots and horsemen."

These references show two things: that chariots were commonly used in Egypt at the time of Joseph and that Joseph's positions included his responsibility for the chariotry; that is why Pharaoh gave him a chariot at his appointment. Up to a decade or two ago, it was thought that the chariots were introduced to Egypt by the Hyksos, who were able to conquer the land with this advanced war machine. Since then, however, it became clear that the Hyksos arrival in Egypt did not take the form of a mass invasion of the land; rather it was a gradual emigration to the eastern delta over more than 100 years, before the newcomers were able to subdue the weak local rulers. At the same time, now that almost all Hyksos sites in the eastern delta have been excavated, no evidence of chariots has ever been found, either in a physical form or in a drawing or a written text. It became now clear that the Egyptian kings of the Eighteenth Dynasty were the first to introduce the chariot.

The situation described in the Joseph story, on the other hand, could not be found during the time of the Hyksos rulers or, indeed, in any earlier period before the time of Amenhotep III. As Alan Richard Schulman, the American philologist, has made clear:

The Eighteenth Dynasty texts testify to the presence of chariotry as a separate military arm only in the protocols of a few individuals. In all other documents of the period known to me . . . no differentiation was made between the infantry and the chariotry. Although it is true that a distinction was made between "horses" and "foot," one may only read into this that the bulk of the soldiers fought on foot, with the remainder employing chariots. All were equally part of the army. . . . However, in the latter Eighteenth Dynasty two ranks are attested, which indicate that such a technical nuance has come into being: Adjutant of the Chariotry, the earliest occurrence of which is known from the Amarna period (of Yuya, who was appointed as Adjutant (Deputy) of His Majesty in the Chariotry as well as Officer for the Horses), and the Standard-Bearer of the Chariot-Warrior. . . . It would thus seem that by this reign (Amenhotep III), chariotry was thought of as a separate entity, and we may assume that the army had been reorganized into the two arms of infantry and chariotry, each with its own organic and administrative components, at about that time.[4]

Thus the first person to be appointed to the position ascribed to Joseph in the Bible was Yuya, the minister to Amenhotep III.

HOW LONG DID THE ISRAELITES LIVE IN EGYPT?

Another reason that persuaded early Egyptologists that the Hyksos period was the right one for Joseph's arrival in Egypt was the fact that they accepted the literary sense of the biblical chronology, which stated that the Israelites' sojourn in Egypt, the time between Joseph's arrival to the country and the Exodus under Moses, lasted 430 years (Exodus 12:40). As the only Egyptian reference of Israel as people, which comes from the fifth year of Pharaoh Merenptah, successor of Ramses II, located them in Canaan around 1219 BCE, scholars went back 430 years and fixed the date of Joseph's arrival, during the very early years of the Hyksos rule. However, the Bible itself gives a different account of the length of this period. Abraham was told by the Lord that his descendents will go to a foreign country for some time, and the fourth generation of those who go shall return to Canaan (Genesis 15:16). The Bible also names only four generations between the time of the Israelite Descent into Egypt and their subsequent Exodus: Levi, Kohath, Amram, and Moses. In this case, if we try to understand the reason behind these two seemingly contradicting accounts, we will realize that there was no contradiction at all. For it seems that the biblical editor arrived at the figure of 430 years by following two steps: he first added the total ages of the four generations: Levi 137, Kohath 133, Amram 137, and Moses 120, which totaled 537 years. He then deducted the 57 years that Levi spent in Canaan before coming to Egypt and the 40 years that Moses is said to have spent in the wilderness of Sinai, and arrived at the figure 430 years.

As we can see, this figure of 430 is the total of the years the four generations lived in Egypt, and not the length of the Israelites' sojourn in that country. Umberto Cassuto, the former Professor of Biblical Studies at the Hebrew University of Jerusalem, explained the reason for this calculation.

> Each generation endured the burden of exile throughout the times of its exile, and its distress was not diminished by the fact that it was shared by another generation during a certain portion of that period; hence in computing the total length of exile suffered, one is justified to some extent in reckoning the ordeal of each generation in its entirety. . . . This figure then cannot be taken to represent the period of time that elapsed between the Israelites' arrival in Egypt and their departure.[5]

By accepting biblical chronology, Egyptologists were looking for the Israelites in Egypt, in the wrong time and wrong place; of course they found no evidence. I followed the opposite path, by fitting the biblical events into the frame of Egyptian chronology. Proving that Yuya and Joseph were one and the same person made the first physical link between Egypt and Israel, and opened the way for the identification of the time and characters of the Exodus.

10

MOSES AND AKHENATEN

Identifying Yuya as being Joseph the Patriarch was the first step to establish a link between Egyptian history and the Bible, opening my way to look for the historical Moses and Exodus. Following the account of Joseph's death at the very end of Genesis, the birth of Moses comes at the start of the following Book of Exodus, with no indication of time lapse. As Joseph is said to have lived to see his great-grandchildren before he died, it seemed reasonable to assume that he must have seen Moses before his death. Now that I have identified Queen Tiye as Joseph's daughter, Freud's suggestion of the Egyptian Moses seemed more possible. Since he had shown the similarity between the religious beliefs of Moses and Akhenaten in his book *Moses and Monotheism,* there has been endless argument about the identity of the first monotheist. On the other hand, while the Bible and the Qu'ran establish Moses as the first monotheist, historical sources identify Akhenaten as the first person who introduced worship of one God (with no image) for all people. Nevertheless, this similarity could not be enough to prove that both characters were one and the same person; for this we have to show that both of them lived at the same historical time in the same geographical location.

THE STORY OF MOSES

According to the Book of Exodus, Moses was born in Egypt to Amram, grandson of Levi, and his aunt Jochebed, daughter of Levi. At the time of his birth, the Israelites were facing hardship, for Pharaoh had forced them to build the store cities of Ramses and Pithom. As Pharaoh had ordered all newborn Hebrew boys to be killed, his mother hid him for three months. When she couldn't hide him any longer, she set him adrift on the water in a small craft of bulrushes coated in pitch. His sister, Miriam, observed the tiny boat until it reached Pharaoh's palace and was picked up by Pharaoh's daughter. Miriam then approached the princess and asked her if she would like a Hebrew woman to nurse the baby. The princess agreed to employ Jochebed as the baby's nurse, and Moses was brought up at Pharaoh's palace.

Thus, according to the biblical account, baby Moses was adopted by the Egyptian royal family. When he grew up to be a young man, Moses went one day for a walk and saw an Egyptian workmaster mistreating a Hebrew; so Moses killed the workmaster. When the news became known, Moses had to flee to south Sinai, where he met a Midianite priest, married his daughter Zipporah, and worked for him as a shepherd for forty years. One day, when he was alone in the desert, Moses encountered the God of Israel, Yahweh, who appeared to him in a "burning bush" at Mount Horeb. Yahweh told him that the Pharaoh who was looking for him has died, and asked him to return to Egypt to confront the new Pharaoh, demanding the release of the Israelites from their bondage. On his way to Egypt, Moses met Aaron, his elder brother, and they went together to the royal palace. At first, Pharaoh refused to let the Israelites leave, so Moses, using his rod by the miraculous power of God, unleashed the Ten Plagues upon Egypt, which eventually persuaded Pharaoh to let the Israelites go.

While Egypt was mourning the deaths of their firstborns, Moses led the children of Israel in their Exodus during the Passover. Pharaoh, in the meantime, changed his mind and went out with his chariots in their pursuit and was able to catch up with them at the Red Sea (or the Sea of Reeds). Here again, with the power of God, Moses used his rod to divide the waters of the sea miraculously, allowing the Israelites to walk through, then the waters returned and drowned Pharaoh and his army. Moses led the Israelites to Mount Sinai (the same as Mount Horeb), where he received the Ten Commandments and gave them to his people, for which reason he became known as the "Lawgiver." Nevertheless, after forty years of wandering in the desert, God informed Moses that he would not be allowed to lead the Israelites into Canaan, and according to the Bible, Moses died at Mount Nebo on the eastern shore of the River Jordan, and God buried him in an unknown grave in the land of Moab in East Jordan.*

Let us now examine the story of Akhenaten and see if we can find any similarity with Moses.

When Yuya was appointed at his official posts, including the Master of the King's Horses and Deputy of the Royal Chariotry, he was also given an Egyptian wife, Tuya, the Mistress of the Harem at Amun's temple at Karnak, who was Amenhotep III's nurse as well. As Tuya's job required her to be living at the royal palace, her daughter Tiye grew up with young Amenhotep. The childhood romance between Amenhotep and Tiye took place as the two children grew up together. However, on coming to the throne Amenhotep had married his infant sister Sitamun, the heiress, to gain the right to the throne according to Egyptian custom.

Nevertheless, in his Year 2 Amenhotep decided to marry Tiye, Yuya's daughter, whom he loved and insisted on making her his Great Royal Wife (queen). To commemorate his marriage with Tiye, the king issued a large scarab and sent copies of it to foreign kings and princes. What shows how much the king loved Tiye is the fact that her name, unlike that of any other queen before, is placed in a royal cartouche, a distinction previously limited to the ruling monarch and is also included in royal titularies. Furthermore, she is represented in art as being of equivalent stature to the king. Although the royal palace at

---

*For more details and references see my books *Moses Pharaoh of Egypt,* published by Grafton in 1990, or *Moses & Akhenaten,* published by Bear & Company in 2002.

the time was located at Memphis, near modern Cairo, Amenhotep III decided to donate the border city of Zarw to Queen Tiye (in the area of modern Kantara east in north Sinai), where he built a summer palace. This seems to be a significant act, since Zarw was the capital town in northern Sinai, at the same area as the biblical land of Goshen. Why should the king donate this city to Tiye unless he wanted his queen to have a chance of living near her father's family, the Israelites, who were not allowed to dwell in the Nile Valley. This is why, although the Israelites were supposed to be living far away from the royal palace, we find them close at the time of Moses's birth, so that the daughter of Pharaoh, his wife in the Qu'ran, could pick the baby out of the water.

Fig. 10.1. Akhenaten's head, from my book Moses and Akhenaten.

A short time after their marriage, Tiye gave birth to a boy, Thutmose. However, he died mysteriously while still a young boy: as soon as his father had appointed him as his heir. Young Thutmose is known to have been educated and trained at Memphis and held the title of the High Priest of Ptah, as did most heirs-apparent during the Eighteenth Dynasty, but then he disappeared suddenly from the scene, more likely not as a result of natural causes. According to Egyptian custom the king could marry as many women as he desired, but the queen, whose children will follow him on the throne, must be his sister the heiress. Although they were forced to accept the king's decision to make Tiye his queen, the priests of Amun would not agree to let her child succeed his father on the throne, for she could not be accepted as the consort of the state god Amun. If her son were to ascend the throne, this would be regarded as forming a new dynasty. Disagreement on this issue started a long conflict between Amhenhotep III and the priests.

In his Year 11, sometime after the death of her son, Amenhotep III dug a pleasure lake for his beloved wife Tiye, in her city of Zarw. To celebrate this occasion, the king issued a special scarab that included the details of this event.

> Year 11, third month of Inundation (first season), day 1, under the majesty of Horus . . . mighty of valor, who smites the Asiatics, King of Upper and Lower Egypt, Neb-Maat-Re, Ron of Re Amenhotep Ruler of Thebes, who is given life, and the Great Royal Wife Tiye, who liveth. His Majesty commanded the making of a lake for the Great King's Wife Tiye, who liveth, in the city of Zarw-kha.

For this occasion, it seems that the royal couple had a second honeymoon at their summer residence in Zarw, and nine months later a new baby was due to be born.

While he loved his queen and didn't wish to upset her, Amenhotep became worried; if she were to give birth to another son, a new confrontation will start again with the priests. Although we don't have any evidence of this, we can understand why the king at that moment would have wanted to get rid of Tiye's new baby, if it proved to be a boy. According to the Bible, the king asked two midwives, Shiphrah and Puah, to kill the child if it was a boy, and keep it if it was a girl. The midwives, however, did not obey the king's orders, and let the boy live. The reason given by the Bible for the king's desire to kill the Hebrew boys is that he feared their fast multiplication. But this is not convincing for two reasons: it is the girls who give birth and help multiplication not the boys, and, as it is well known, Israelite children follow their mother not their father. Consequently we can understand how Amenhotep III, motivated by the possible threat to the dynasty, and more confrontation with the priests, could have instructed the midwives to kill Tiye's child secretly if it proved to be a boy. The Talmud account confirms that it was the survival of Moses that Pharaoh wanted to prevent, not all the Israelite children. Once he knew that Moses had been born, his attempt to kill the Israelite boys was abandoned.

Following Freud's argument, Moses should have been born inside the royal palace, which, by the way, is the same sense of the Qu'ranic account. However, although the child's father, Amehotep III, was the king of Egypt, his mother, Queen Tiye, was the daughter of Joseph the Israelite. Because there was a danger on his life, his mother, Queen Tiye, sent him away across the palace lake, to the safekeeping of her Israelite relations at nearby Goshen. This is how Akhenaten, the second son of Amenhotep III and Queen Tiye, was born at the frontier city of Zarw, about 1394 BCE. What makes the threat on Akhenaten's life at his birth more believable is the fact that later on he adopted the title of "The Long Living." At the same time, while still alive, Akhenaten represented himself as an Osiris in many statues, which can only be made for dead kings.

Akhenaten was born in an era of peace and prosperity in Egypt. A combination of diplomacy, judicious marriages, and equally judicious use of gold had secured a balance of power, at least temporarily, between Egypt and the neighboring state of Mitanni, the Hittites of Asia Minor, the Assyrians, and the Babylonians of Mesopotamia. Palestine and Syria, conquered by Thutmose III in the middle of the fifteenth century BCE, posed no threat; the southern frontier had been secured up to and beyond the Nile's Fourth Cataract. Luxuries from the Levant and the Aegean world poured into Egypt on a greater scale than ever before. More land was brought under cultivation, art flourished, prosperous state officials and priests enjoyed the pleasures of new townhouses and country villas with large estates. How the common people fared is less clear, but they must have benefited from the general prosperity and the state projects that offered alternative employment during the long summer droughts.

Throughout the country, new temples were founded by Amenhotep III, old ones restored. One of the biggest temporal projects was the king's splendid palace, the Malkata, in western Thebes, opposite modern Luxor, with an imposing mortuary temple beside it. Thebes was also the seat of the state god, Amun-Re. While ancient cults of other gods continued to flourish locally, the cult of Amun-Re had received, and continued to receive, such favorable royal treatment—generous endowment for the great temple of Karnak at Thebes, magnificent gifts of land and gold—that it had become virtually an arm of the state executive. Yet there was already a hint in the air of the enormous religious upheaval that lay ahead.

Fearing for her son's life, Tiye kept her baby away from the royal residence at Memphis and Thebes. Akhenaten's absence from the royal residence during his early years can only be explained by the fact that, during this period of his life, he was living at Zarw and Heliopolis. Zarw was the military border city in northern Sinai, surrounded by lakes and an ancient branch of the Nile. It was the capital city of the area known as Goshen in the Bible, where the Israelites were allowed to settle. It is from his behavior and the kind of knowledge he seemed to have acquired at the time of his arrival at Thebes that we have to guess at where Akhenaten most probably passed the greater part of his childhood. His appearance does not suggest that he had any physical training, contrary to the custom among Eighteenth-Dynasty kings, and he is never shown hunting lions or other wild animals. Nor is he depicted smiting an enemy or leading his army in combat.

At the same time, as many elements of Akhenaten's new religion had their ritual origin in the solar worship of Heliopolis, this points to his having had some of his education in this city, especially as Anen, Queen Tiye's brother, was a priest of Re at Heliopolis.

It was only after he had grown up as a young man that Akhenaten was finally allowed to take up residence at Thebes, the capital city in Upper Egypt and the principal center of worship of the state god, Amun. By this time the health of his father had begun to deteriorate and Tiye's influence had increased correspondingly. As her son reached his midteens, Tiye took the precaution of ensuring his right to the throne by marrying him to Nefertiti, his half-sister, daughter of Amenhotep III and his sister Sitamun, and therefore the rightful heiress. Later, Horemheb, the last ruler of the Eighteenth Dynasty, had to marry Nefertiti's sister, Munezmat, to gain the right to the throne.

As a further step toward ensuring her son's right to the throne, Tiye subsequently persuaded Amenhotep III to appoint him as his coregent at Thebes. Thus his marriage to the new heiress allowed his father to appoint him as his coregent, with a special emphasis on Nefertiti's role in order to placate the priests. Akhenaten's appearance at Thebes does not seem to have occurred before Year 20 of his father, Amehotep III, when the evidence of the wine-jar seal has been interpreted as "the true king's son, Amenhotep," indicates that he had a palace there. William C. Hayes, the American Egyptologist, comments on this inscription: "The King's son, Amenhotep, referred to here was in all probability the future King Amenhotep IV before his elevation to the coregency, which is thought to have taken place in or about Year 28 of Amenhotep III." Akhenaten is believed to have been about sixteen years old at the time. Going back sixteen years before the start of coregency in Year 28, we arrive at Year 12 of his father's rule for his birth, a year after the pleasure lake was dug in Zarw, which dates Akhenaten's birth in 1394 BCE.

On his accession to the throne as coregent, Akhenaten took the names Nefer-khepru-re Waenre Amenhotep—that is, Amenhotep IV—and from his very first year provoked the priests with his aggressive attitude. He had barely assumed his new position when he used some of the wealth amassed by his father to build at Thebes a large new temple to Aten—a God for the world, not just for Egyptians—within the precincts of the existing Amun temple at Karnak. He snubbed the traditional priests by not inviting them to any of the festivities in the

Map of Egypt during the time of the Empire, 16th–12th centuries BCE

Fig. 10.2. Egypt during the time of the empire.

early part of his coregency and, in his fourth year, when he celebrated his *sed* festival or jubilee—usually, but not necessarily, a rejuvenation celebration that marked Year 30 of a monarch's reign—he banned all deities but his own God from the occasion. Twelve months later he made a further break with tradition by changing his name to Akhenaten in honor of his new deity.

At Thebes, during the early years of his coregency, Nefertiti was active in supporting her husband and more prominent than Akhenaten in official occasions as well as on all monuments and inscriptions. However, the climate of hostility that surrounded Akhenaten at the time of his birth surfaced again after his appointment as coregent. The reason this time was the young coregent's new provoking monotheistic beliefs. Akhenaten, whose religious ideas were already well developed, offended the Amunite priesthood from the start. The Amun priesthood did not hesitate to oppose his appointment as coregent, and openly challenged Amenhotep III's decision. In response to their opposition, the young coregent decided to build a temple to his new God, Aten, within Amun's Karnak complex in Thebes. To the resentful Egyptian establishment Aten was seen as a challenger who would replace the powerful state god Amun and not come under his domination. The Memphite inscription of his father's Year 30 had sought to defend his action in "placing the male offspring upon the throne," suggesting that there had been opposition—undoubtedly from the Amun priesthood and the nobility—to his action in securing the inheritance for his son. In the tense climate that prevailed, Tiye and her husband seem to have been able to persuade their son to leave Thebes and look for new ground for his new God, so the situation calmed down, following Akhenaten's departure while Amenhotep ruled alone in Thebes.

MOVE TO AMARNA

As all cities in Egypt were already under the protection of some deities, Akhenaten looked for new ground to establish his new city for his own God, Aten. Going downstream, his boat came to an area in Middle Egypt on the east bank of the Nile, 312 km (194 miles) south of modern Cairo, which had not been inhabited before. It was a desert site surrounded on three sides by cliffs and to the west by the Nile. At this point the cliffs of the high desert recede from the river, leaving a great semicircle about eight miles long and three miles broad. The clean yellow sand slopes gently down to the river. It was here that Akhenaten built his new capital, Akhetaten "The Horizon of Aten," at the modern site of Tell el-Amarna, where his followers could be free to worship their monotheistic God.

Huge boundary stelae, marking the limits of the city and recording the story of its foundation, were carved in the surrounding cliffs. The first of them dates from about the fourth year of the coregency when Akhenaten had decided upon the site. On some of these boundary stelae, fixed before the start of the building of his new city of Amarna in his Year 4, Akhenaten refers to what appears to be open opposition he had faced prior to that date:

> For, as Father Hor-Aten liveth . . . priests more evil are they than those things, which I heard unto Year 4, [more evil are they] than [those things] which I have heard in year . . . more evil are they than those things which King . . . [heard], more evil are they than those things which Menkheberure (Thutmose IV) heard.

Akhenaten is here referring to hostile comments he heard about himself prior to Year 4, not only that two kings who preceded him, his father and grandfather, had been subject to similar verbal criticism. A later set of stelae date from the sixth year and define both the city on the east bank and a large area of agricultural land on the bank opposite, apparently with a view to making the new capital self-supporting if it ever came under siege. One of the stelae proclamations states:

> As my father Aten lives, I shall make Akhetaten (Amarna) for Aten my father in this place. I shall not make him Akhetate[n] south of it, north of it, west of it or east of it. And Akhetaten extends from the southern stela as far as the northern stela, measured between stela and stela on the eastern mountain, likewise from the

south-west stela to the north-west stela on the western mountain of Akhetaten. And the area between these four stelae is
Akhetaten itself; it belongs to *Aten my father,* mountains, deserts,
meadows, islands, high ground and low ground, land, water, villages,
men, beasts, and all things, which Aten my father shall bring into
existence eternally forever. I shall not forget this oath, which I have
made to Aten my father eternally forever.

A reiteration of his vows, made to his new capital, was added in his
eighth year, which is thought the most likely time that the king, Queen
Nefertiti, and their six daughters—Merytaten, Meketaten, Ankhsenpa-
aten, Nefereneferu-aten the younger, Neferneferure, and Setepenre, all
born before Year 9 of the king's reign—took up residence.

The building of the new city started in his Year 4 and ended in
Year 8; however, he and his family moved from Thebes to Amarna in
Year 6. A fine city it was. Akhenaten was a capital city possessed of
both dignity and architectural harmony. Its main streets ran parallel to
the Nile with the most important of them, the King's Way, connecting
the city's most prominent buildings, including the King's House where
Akhenaten and his family lived their private family life. To the south
of the house was the king's private Temple to Aten. The Great Temple
of Aten, a huge building constructed on an east-west axis, lay less than
a quarter of a mile to the north along the King's Way. It was entered
through a pylon from the highway and a second entrance gave access
to a hypostyle hall called the House of Rejoice of Aten. The house of
the high priest Panehesy lay outside the enclosure's southeast corner.
Akhenaten gave tombs, gouged out of the face of the cliffs surrounding
his city, to those nobles who had rallied to him. In the reliefs, which the
nobles carved for themselves in these tombs—showing Akhenaten with
his queen and family dispensing honors and largesse, worshipping in the
temple, driving in his chariot, dining, and drinking—Queen Nefertiti
is depicted as having equal stature with the king and her names are
enclosed in a cartouche. Like her mother-in-law, Queen Nefertiti enjoyed
a prominence that had not existed in the past. Akhenaten spoke of his

wife as being: "Fair of Face, Joyous with the Double Plume, Mistress of Happiness, Endowed with Favor, at hearing whose voice one rejoices, Lady of Grace, Great of Love, whose disposition cheers the Lord of the Two Lands." Here in their new home, Akhenaten, his Queen Nefertiti, and their six daughters lived with their nobles and officials worshipping Aten. Here also a son was born to the royal couple in Year 7, and they named him Tutankh-aten, "the Living Image of Aten," who later changed his name to Tutankgamun.

MOSES'S GOD

Before the time of Moses, the patriarchs identified their God in a variety of terms, all of which were names of ancient Canaanite deities, such as: El, Elohim, Yahweh, 'Elyon, 'Olam, Shaddai. The name Elohim (the plural of Eloho meaning "a god"), which is used in the Bible more than 2,000 times, is usually translated in English as God; while the name YHWH (Jehovah), which is understood to mean "I am" and is referred to as the "Tetragrammaton," also occurs 6,000 times in the Bible. However, since Moses delivered the Ten Commandments, the name Jehovah was forbidden to be pronounced, except by the priests and in certain limited occasions, and was replaced by Adonai, my Lord, the same name of Akhenaten's God. As the Egyptian T becomes D in Hebrew with the change of vowels, Egyptian "Aten" becomes "Adon" in Hebrew, as Sigmund Freud correctly noted.

AKHENATEN'S GOD

Although from the time of his appearance in Thebes, when he was about sixteen years old, Akhenaten seemed to have already developed his monotheistic beliefs, it took him about ten more years to recognize the final nature of Aten. In his Year 1, Akhenaten was shown worshipping his God at the quarry of Gebel Silsila in Nubia, where he called himself the "first prophet" of "Re-Harakhti, Rejoicing-in-the Horizon, in his name Shu (beam of light) which is in Aten." At this early stage the deity was represented as a human shape, either with the head of a falcon surmounted with the solar disc or as a winged disc, presented in the conventional artistic style. Between the King's Year 4 and Year 5 a new style of art started to appear, part of it realistic, part distinguished by an exaggeration of expression. There was also a new representation of the deity. A disc at the top of royal scenes extended its rays toward the king and queen, and the rays end in their hands, which hold the ankh, the Egyptian symbol of life, to the noses of the king and queen, a privilege, which only they enjoy, as they were the major figures in Aten's cult. At the same time the name and epithet of Aten were placed inside two cartouches, matching the manner in which the ruling king's names were written.

In Year 6 Aten was given a new epithet, "Celebrator of Jubilees," jubilees that coincided significantly with those of the king. Then, toward the end of Year 9 the name of Aten received its new form to rid it of any therio-anthropomorphic and panetheistic ideas that may have clung to it. The falcon symbol that had been used to spell the word "Re-Harakhti" was changed to abstract signs giving an equivalent "Re, Ruler of the Horizon," while a phrase in the second cartouche was also altered, ridding it of the word, "Shu," for light, which was also representation of the old Egyptian god of the void. This was replaced by other signs. The new form of Aten's name read:

"Re, the living Ruler of the Horizon, *in his name* (aspect) of the light which is in Aten."

Here we find another connection between Akhenaten and Moses. For although Moses's father was called Amram (Imran in Egyptian), the name of Akhenaten's father was Amenhotep. However, in the God's second cartouche, Aten's name is given as Im-r-n (Imran), which has been translated as "in his name." As Akhenaten regarded Aten to be his divine father, Imran became the name of his father. For this reason, the city of Akhetaten is called Amarna. Contrary to the general belief, the name Amarna does not derive from a Muslim Arab tribe that settled in the area in modern times. No evidence of such event exists, while Amarna is part of the Minya Province, whose population is mostly Christian Copts. The name "Amarna" derives from Aten's name as found in his second cartouche, Im-r-n. Another similarity between Akhenaten and Moses is the close relation they both had with the Levite priests. The Bible tells us little about the origins of the Levites who played an important role in the Exodus account. In his book *Moses and Monotheism,* Sigmund Freud suggested that the Levites "were the Egyptian followers of Moses." To support this view, he pointed out that only among the Levites do Egyptian names occur later. What makes Freud's argument more acceptable is the fact that the name of Meryre, the High Priest of Aten at Amana, is the Hebrew equivalent of the name Merari, who is described in Genesis 46:11 as one of the sons of Levi. Similarly, the name of Panehesy, who was the Chief Servitor of Aten in Amarna, is the Hebrew equivalent of Phinehas, the son of Eleazar and grandson of Aaron (Exodus 6:25), in whose family the priesthood was to remain. It is, therefore, a possibility that we are dealing here with the same people who served Akhenaten at Amarna and then accompanied him to exile in Sinai. Again, across the river from Amarna, on the west bank of the Nile, we find the modern city of Mal-Lawi. As Egyptian W becomes V in Hebrew, this name becomes Mal-Levi, which literary means "The City of Levi." This could only be explained by the fact that the Levites, who held priestly positions with Moses, held the same positions at Amarna, which can also confirm Manetho's Osarseph account, when he includes priests among the followers of the rebel leader.

Akhenaten regarded himself as Aten's channel of communication and only he had the power to interpret the divine will. In the longer hymn to Aten, thought to have been composed by Akhenaten himself, a poetic passage credits Aten with the creation of all the phenomena of the universe and asserts that all creatures exist only by virtue of the sun's rising and infusing them with life each morning. Traditionally, the ruling Pharaoh was regarded as being the head of the priesthood, head of the army, and head of the administration of the Two Lands of Egypt. When he rejected the gods of Egypt, Akhenaten ceased to be head of the priesthood and the temples of Egypt were no longer under his control. He also had no control over the running of the country while his father was still alive. But, from the time he moved to Amarna,

Akhenaten relied completely on the army's support for protection and, possibly, as a future safeguard against the confrontation that would be inevitable once his father died and he became sole ruler.

When we compare Akhenaten's teaching about his God, from inscriptions at Aten's temple and Amarna tombs with that of Moses's in the Bible, we find that the main point both characters is preaching for one universal God with no image, the universal King who created the world:

> Hear, O Israel, The Lord (Adonai) our God, the Lord is the one. (Deuteronomy 6:4)
>
> The living Aten, is none other than He. . . . Who Himself gave birth to Himself . . . He who decrees life, the Lord of sunbeams.
>
> In the beginning God created the heavens and the earth. (Genesis 1:1)
>
> The world came forth from Thy [Aten] hand. . . . Thou . . . creator of months and maker of days, and reckoner of hours.
>
> The Lord shall reign for ever and ever. (Exodus 15:18)
>
> Thou create the earth when Thou were afar, namely men, cattle, all flocks, and everything on earth which moves with legs, or which is up above flying with wings, the foreign countries of Syria (north) and Kush (south), and the land of Egypt. . . . Everyone has his food, and his lifetime is reckoned; and similarly their languages are wholly separate in form. For their colors are different, for Thou hast made foreign peoples different.

ATEN RULES ALONE

On the death of his father, when Akhenaten became sole ruler in Year 12 of the coregency, the king made more serious decisions. As Aten was the only God, Akhenaten, as his sole son and prophet, could not allow other gods to be worshiped in his domain. Now he took his ideas to their logical conclusion by abolishing worship of any gods throughout Egypt except Aten. Under his rule, Akhenaten's subjects were totally committed by the king to worship Aten alone, as he closed all the temples except those of Aten, dispersed the priests, and ordered the names of other deities to be expunged from inscriptions throughout the country. Units were dispatched to excise the names of the ancient gods wherever they were found written or engraved, a course that can only have created mounting new opposition to his already rejected authority.

Akhenaten gave orders to his troops instructing them to close all the temples, confiscate estates, and sack the priests, leaving only Aten's temples throughout the country. This persecution was supervised by the army. Each time a squad of workmen entered a temple or tomb to destroy the name of Amun, it was supported by a squad of soldiers who came to see that the royal decree was carried out without opposition. As he did not have enough support from his people, who couldn't understand his idea of an abstract God with no image, the king had to rely completely on his army to enforce his orders.

Akhenaten did not have the usual military training of the royal princes, and he alone of the Eighteenth Dynasty kings is not represented as an active participant in horsemanship and archery, in which his forebears excelled; nevertheless, he seems to have been at pains to emphasize his military authority. In the majority of the representations, he is shown wearing the Blue Crown or the short Nubian wig, rather than the traditional crowns of Lower and Upper Egypt. His use of military headgear on every possible occasion must have been intended to identify him in the minds of his people as a military leader. If we take the reliefs from the tombs of the nobles at their face value, Amarna was virtually an armed camp. Everywhere we see processions and parades of soldiers, infantry, and chariotry with their massed standards. It is also notable that the military garrison of Amarna had detachments of foreign auxiliaries of Asiatics and Africans in addition to Egyptian units. It was mainly the loyalty of the army under General Aye's leadership that kept Akhenaten in power in the uneasy years since he came to the throne as sole ruler upon the death of his father. Aye, his maternal uncle, the husband of Tiy, his and Nefertiti's nurse, held posts among the highest in the infantry and the chariotry, which were also held by his father Yuya. Aye was certainly the power behind Akhenaten's throne from the time of the death of Amenhotep III. However, unlimited loyalty from the army could not reasonably be expected; after all, the officers and soldiers themselves believed in the gods whose images they were ordered to destroy. A conflict arose. Aye seem to have realized the danger—Aten, the Amarna family, and their followers were under threat—a compromise was the wisest course to follow. When Akhenaten refused to compromise, Aye advised him to abdicate in favor of his young son Tutankhaten, later to be called Tutankhamun, and go to exile in Sinai.

MILITARY COUP

Archaeological evidence to support the conclusion that Akhenaten was forced to abdicate the throne by a military coup came to light as Alain-Pierre Zivie, the French archaeologist, discovered the tomb of Maya. In the Saqqara region, ten miles south of Cairo, Zivie uncovered the tomb of Maya, Tutankhamun's wet-nurse. When first found, the tomb was almost completely full of mummified cats, placed there almost 1,000 years after the original burial. However, on the wall he found a scene depicting Maya protecting the king, who is sitting on her knee. The inscriptions describe her as "the royal nanny who breast-fed the Pharaoh's body." Behind her, to the left, are six officials representing Tutankhamun's cabinet, two above, and four below, each with different facial characteristics. Although none of the officials are named, Zivie was able to suggest their identities from their appearance and insignia of office. With one exception, all are military men, four of whom sat on the throne of Egypt after the death of Tutankhamun. Zivie recognized the two above as Aye, who succeeded Tutankhamun (his great-uncle); and Horemheb, last ruler of the Eighteenth Dynasty, who followed Aye. The four below are Pa-Ramses, the first Pharaoh of the Nineteenth Dynasty; his son, Seti I, who succeeded his father on the throne; General Nakht Min, thought to be relative of Aye, who disappeared later; and Maya, who was a civilian minister for finance. The six officials also named Maya, the wet nurse, as a treasurer.

This is the first time in Egyptian history that we find the king's cabinet composed almost totally of army generals, who could have gained their positions of power, and later the throne, only as the result of a military coup. It is clear that in his Year 17 Akhenaten faced an army rebellion led by Horemheb, Pa-Ramses, and Seti. As General Aye, supported by General Nakht Min, was unable to crush the rebellion, they made a deal with the generals to allow the abdication of Akhenaten and the appointment of his young son Tutankhamun as the new ruler over Egypt. Akhenaten, no doubt reluctantly, accepted the situation. The place he chose for exile was the wilderness of Sinai.

Nine years later, Aye succeeded Tutankhamun after his great nephew's early death, only to disappear mysteriously, along with Nakht Min, following a reign of only four years. Horemheb then seized power and appointed the other two leaders of the military coup, Pa-Ramses and Seti, as viziers and commander generals of the army, thus creating the situation that enabled them to come to the throne eventually as the first two Pharaohs of the new Nineteenth Dynasty.

WAS MOSES A KING?

While we know from the Old Testament that Moses was brought up in the royal palaces, it does not suggest that he ever succeeded the throne. Yet the story of Moses in the Talmud, the compilation of Hebrew laws and legends, dating from the early centuries CE and regarded as second only to the Old Testament as an authoritative source of the early history of the Jews, contains some details not to be found in the Bible, and often parallels Manetho's account. One of the details is that Moses became a king and had to abdicate the throne, exactly like Akhenaten.

According to the Talmud, Moses grew into a handsome lad, dressed royally, was honored by the people, and seemed in all things of royal lineage. However, at about the age of eighteen he was forced to flee after, on a visit to Goshen, he came across an Egyptian smiting one of his Israelite brethren and slew him. The Talmud goes on to relate that at about this time there was a rebellion against the king of Ethiopia (Nubia). The king there had appointed one of Pharaoh's advisers to be his representative in his absence while he marched at the head of his army to defeat the rebels. Pharaoh's adviser, however, betrayed the king and usurped the power he was supposed to protect, while the king was absent. On his return to his country the king found the gates of the city closed against him, so he embarked on war against the usurper that lasted nine years.

Moses, according to the Talmud story, was one of those who fought on the side of the Ethiopian king as, after fleeing from Egypt, he did not go to Sinai but to Ethiopia. For his bravery and courage, Moses became a great favorite with the king and his companions with the result that, when the king died, they appointed him as their king. Moses, who, according to the Talmud, was made king "in the hundred and fifty-seventh year after Israel went down into Egypt," inspired the army with his courage, and the city eventually fell to him. The account goes on: "the Ethiopians placed Moses upon their throne and set the crown of State upon his head, and they gave him the widow of their king for a wife."

Moses reigned in justice and righteousness but, after nine years,

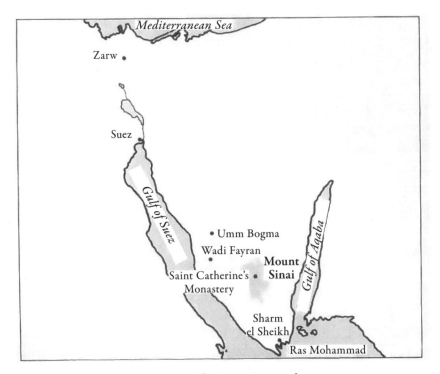

Fig. 10.3. The Sinai Peninsula.

the Queen of Ethiopia, Adonith [Aten-it in Egyptian], who wished her own son by the dead king to rule, said to the people: "Why should this stranger continue to rule over you?" The people, however, would not vex Moses, whom they loved, by such a proposition; but Moses resigned voluntarily the power, which they had given him, and departed from their land and went to Sinai.

Where did the rabbis obtain these facts in the Talmud? They can hardly have invented them and, indeed, had no reason to do so. Like the accounts of Manetho, the Talmudic stories contain many distortions and accretions arising from the fact that they were transmitted orally for a long time before finally being set down in writing. Yet one can sense that behind these stories there must have been genuine historical events that had been suppressed from the official accounts of both Egypt and Israel but had survived in the memories of the generations.

EXILE IN SINAI

There are many indications that Akhenaten spent his exile years in Sinai. Sinai Peninsula is in the form of a triangle with its apex to the south between the two arms of the Red Sea, the Gulf of Suez, and the Gulf of Aqaba. At its northern base runs the road of Horus from Egypt to Asia, stating from Kantarah, east of the Suez Canal, to Gaza, along the Mediterranean coastline. To the south of this low northern land is a lofty limestone plateau, crossed by only a few narrow passes. The southern triangle, between the two arms of the Red Sea, is a mountain mass including Mount Sinai or Mount Horeb (modern name, Gebel Musa, which means the Mount of Moses). En route from the eastern Nile Delta through the valleys, before arriving at Mount Sinai we come to another important site, Sarabit el-Khadim, a mountain area with many turquoise mines.

During the reign of Amenhotep III, the treasury had been placed for three generations in the hands of one family, that of Pa-Nehes the Levite. Akhenaten himself also appointed Panehesy, a descendant of Pa-Nehes, as his chancellor and Chief Servitor of Aten in his temple at Amarna as well as the Servitor of the King in the temple. Thus the Levite family of Pa-Nehes, which does not seem to have had any priestly connection before, was not only involved in Akhenaten's government, but in his worship as well. This family was also responsible for the mining expeditions sent to Sarabit el-Khadem in southern Sinai. It would therefore have been normal for them to suggest Sarabit as a place for Akhenaten's exile where they would be able to protect him and give him support. Sarabit offered the best, if not the only, location for Akhenaten's exile—as it was regarded as a holy place including a temple, close to another holy place, Mount Sinai, away from Egyptian control, where he could meditate and develop his religious ideas.

In the early years of the nineteenth century, Flinders Petrie, the British archaeologist, led an expedition into Sinai where he recorded what he was able to find of ancient inscriptions. The resulting evidence showed that the Egyptians had sent expeditions to the mountain of Sinai since early dynastic times, mainly for the purpose of mining turquoise. On the high peak of Sarabit, 2,600 feet above sea level, a shrine was constructed; originally in a cave, by the time of the New Kingdom it had been extended outside and reached a total length of 230 feet. This temple was dedicated to Hathor, the local deity. Petrie found fragments of a limestone stela at Sarabit made by Ramses I at the start of the Nineteenth Dynasty. Although the stela is not actually dated, this poses no problem, as Ramses I ruled for less than two years. What is surprising about the stela is that in its inscription Ramses I describes himself as "the ruler of all that Aten embraces." Of this unexpected reappearance of the fallen Aten, Petrie commented: "To find the Aten mentioned thus after the ruthless Amunism of Horemheb is remarkable. Hitherto the latest mention of it was under King Aye."

The name of Aten had been missing for thirteen years during the reign of Horemheb: now in the time of his successor, Ramses I, the hated God has appeared, not in Egypt proper but in Sinai. Usually Pharaoh gives his blessing and makes his offering to the deity of the area he is visiting. Was Aten still being worshipped at Sarabit and why? This stela, made more than a quarter of a century after Akhenaten's fall from power, also features the Amarna realistic style: the portion, which is carefully wrought, and in the dress resembles the work of Akhenaten.

This was not the only surprising discovery made by Petrie relating

Akhenaten to Sarabit. Inside the temple he found a dark green head, executed in the Amarna style, of a statuette of Queen Tiye, Akhenaten's mother. The complete statuette must have been about a foot high, which makes it easy to carry. Who took Tiye's statue to Sarabit and why? "It is strange that this remotest settlement of Egypt has preserved her portrait for us, unmistakably named by her cartouche in the midst of the crown," Petrie remarked. "The haughty dignity of the face is blended with a fascinating directness and personal appeal. The delicacy of the surfaces round the eye and over the cheek shows the greatest delicacy in handling. The curiously drawn-down lips with their fullness and yet delicacy, their disdain without malice, are evidently modeled in all truth from the life."[1]

Petrie found evidence indicating that the rituals performed in the temple at Sarabit were of Semitic nature. He found a bed of clean white ash under a considerable portion of the temple, amounting to more than fifty tons, which he took to represent the remains of burnt sacrifices over a long period. This practice is known from the Bible to have been Israelite. Petrie also found three rectangular tanks and a circular basin, placed to be used at four locations in successive halls leading to the holy of holies area.

BACK FROM EXILE

The death of Horemheb left Egypt without a legitimate heir to the Eighteenth Dynasty. General Pa-Ramses, by now an old man, therefore prepared to claim the throne for himself as the first ruler of the Nineteenth Dynasty. Akhenaten, who had been hiding in his exile in Sinai, decided to return and reclaim his throne from Ramses. He made his way back to the border city of Zarw, where Ramses had his residence, to challenge the new king as the rightful heir to the Thutmose Dynasty. The only evidence Akhenaten had to offer in order to prove his right to the throne was his royal scepter, which is described in the Bible as Moses's rod. For some of the most fascinating sections of the biblical story of Moses are those dealing with the magical power of his rod. When the Lord asked him to leave Sinai and return to Egypt in order to liberate the

Israelites, Moses was not sure that neither they nor Pharaoh would listen to him or believe in him. To strengthen his position, the Lord asked him to use his rod, to confirm his identity as the messenger of God.

In religion and matters of faith, we can accept miraculous and supernatural events; however, in history this is not possible. We can accept seeing Superman in the movies, but we don't expect to find him in real life. How could Moses, a Bedouin shepherd coming from Sinai, be allowed not only to enter the royal palace, but to confront Pharaoh as well and challenge him on his authority? Would an ordinary person be allowed to meet Pharaoh in his own palace, and threaten him with some mysterious power? In real history, if at all Moses was able to challenge Pharaoh in his own palace, he would have been sent to prison or even executed on the spot. On the other hand, magic implies the existence of a realm of power that transcends Nature and the deities. It is an attempt to influence events by occult means and is, therefore, in complete contrast with the monotheistic religion of both Moses and Akhenaten. Ancient man believed that he was able to influence the mysterious forces surrounding him by means of magical rituals or utterances. This was true also of the Egyptians, who had special priests to practice these arts. They believed that they could achieve their desired end by such means. Magic was employed particularly to protect the dead on their journey through the underworld, and to ensure their return for a second life. At the same time, the Bible opposes all kinds of magic. Any belief in its efficacy is seen as contradicting the Israelite belief in the exclusive and supreme rule of one God, whose will cannot be influenced by human means. Akhenaten also rejected all kinds of magic. Even the practices, dear to the Egyptians, relating to the spells of the Book of the Dead, that guaranteed a safe journey through the underworld, as well as the trial of the deceased before Osiris—the dead king of the dead—and his tribunal found no place in Akhenaten's religion.

The subsequent confrontation between Moses and the Egyptian magicians and sorcerers described in chapter seven of the Book of Exodus, explained as miracles in the case of Moses and magic in the case of the Egyptians, is not really convincing as both sides were said

to have employed the same methods. When we examine the acts said
to have been performed by Moses to establish his identity we find that
they were largely related to some old Egyptian rituals that kings used
to perform in their Sed festivals for the purpose of rejuvenating their
power. The biblical account reads as follows.

> And Moses and Aaron went in unto Pharaoh, and they did so as
> the Lord had commanded: and Aaron cast down his rod before
> Pharaoh, and before his servants, and it became a serpent. Then
> Pharaoh also called the wise man and the sorcerers: now the magi-
> cians of Egypt, they also did in like manner with their enchant-
> ments. For they cast down every man his rod, and they became
> serpents: but Aaron's rod swallowed up their rods. And he hard-
> ened Pharaoh's heart that he hearkened not unto them; as the
> Lord had said. (Exodus 7:10–13)

What confirms this section of the biblical narration must have
gone through much editing is the fact that, not only does it imply
that Aaron rather than Moses performed the rod scene, it also lacks
many details found in the same scene in the Qu'ran. According to
the Qu'ran, Moses informed Pharaoh that he was a messenger sent
from God demanding the release of the Children of Israel to go with
him. When Pharaoh demanded a sign, Moses, not Aaron, threw his
rod, and it became a snake. Pharaoh's officials said to the Israelites:
this is a well-versed magician who wants to get you out of your land,
and advised Pharaoh to send for all the well-versed sorcerers in the
land who are able to confront Moses. The Egyptian magicians (wise
men) came to Pharaoh and asked to be rewarded when they won; and
Pharaoh agreed. When they threw their rods, it bewitched the eyes of
the audience and struck terror in them, but God inspired Moses to
throw his rod, which swallowed their falsehood. Seeing the power of
Moses's rod, the magicians kneeled down in front of him in adoration
and announced: We believe in the Lord of Moses and Aaron. This
angered Pharaoh who threatened to cut off their hands and feet and
crucify them all (Sura 7:104–24).

Here we have a real debate between Moses and Pharaoh, where the wise men of Egypt accept Moses's authority as soon as they see him performing the scepter ritual. For Egyptian kings used to have a collection of rods representing different aspects of their authority, one of which is the scepter of the king's power, a rod in the shape of a serpent either made of or covered with brass. Now, the Hebrew word used in the Bible to indicate Moses's rod is *nahash,* which has the double meaning of "serpent" and "brass." The Haggadah, the legendary part of the Talmud, confirms that royal character of Moses's rod: "The rod which Moses used . . . was shaped and engraved in the image of a scepter." During the Sed festival, celebrated by Egyptian kings, including Akhenaten, to rejuvenate their power, it was the custom to take part in rituals that included the serpent rod performed by Moses in front of Pharaoh. In the tomb of Kheruef, one of Queen Tiye's stewards, a throne scene shows the queen with her husband, Amenhotep III. Under the dais of the throne we see Kheruef and other officials, each holding something that he is about to hand to the king so that he can use it during his Sed festival celebrations of his Year 30. The fourth of these officials holds a curved scepter with serpent's head on his left. So, in the course of their Sed festival celebrations, Egyptian kings performed rituals that corresponded to the serpent rod ritual performed by Moses; and in performing it, Moses was not using magic but seeking to establish his royal authority.

The correct interpretation of these magic accounts in the Bible points to the fact that Akhenaten must have taken his royal rod with him when he was forced to abdicate the throne and leave for exile in Sinai. When the magicians saw the scepter of royal authority and Akhenaten performing the royal rituals of the Sed festival, the wise men bowed at the knee to him, confirming his right to the throne. However, Ramses used his military office to crush the rebels. It was then that Akhenaten was forced to flee from Egypt at the head of his followers, including his mother's Israelite relatives.

THE NAME MOSES

Akhenaten's name, objects, and memory survived until the end of
the reign of King Aye, the last of the Amarna kings, who followed
Tutankhamun on the throne. However, with the accession of Horemheb
and the Ramesside kings who succeeded him, all standing monuments
of Amarna were pulled down and worship of Aten was forbidden.
Horemheb and his successors also ensured that all memory of Akhenaten
was wiped out of Egypt's official records, even to having his name and
the names of the three Amarna kings who succeeded him erased from
the official king lists. It seems that the name Moses, found in the Bible
and the Qu'ran, was rather a codename of Egyptian origin such as "Ptah-
mose" and "Thut-mose." We also find examples of the name "Mose" used
on its own as a pronoun belonging to the New Kingdom, which started
with the Eighteenth Dynasty. Nevertheless, private texts referring to
events that had taken place during Akhenaten's reign, while not mentioning him by name, used synonyms referring to him as "The Fallen One of
Akhetaten (Amarna)" and "The Rebel of Akhetaten."

A papyrus in the Berlin Museum, dating most probably from the
time of the Nineteenth Dynasty, contains remains of a letter that gives
the date of someone's death during the period of Akhenaten's rule in
the following form: "he died in Year 9 of the rebel." As well as avoiding
mention of his name, this text shows us that he was regarded as an out-
law by the Ramessides that would justify all the vengeful actions they
were taking against his memory. In a legal text from the tomb of Mose
during the Nineteenth Dynasty, in referring to events that had taken
place during Akhenaten's reign, some of the witnesses used another
expression: "Pa-kherw-n Akhetaten," which literally means "the fallen
of Akhetaten."

"Mose" was used in a legal sense during the Nineteenth Dynasty
to indicate the heir who inherits a land of a dead person. When the
Egyptian authorities forbade any mention of Akhenaten's name, it
seems that an alternative had to be used when his followers refer to him.
Faced with the accusation that Akhenaten was not the real heir to the
throne, his followers must have called him "mose, the son and heir," to

indicate that he was the legitimate son of Amenhotep III and the rightful heir to his father's throne.

THE TEN COMMANDMENTS

The Ten Commandments given by the Lord God of Moses to the Israelites in Sinai are clearly in an Egyptian tradition and would seem to have common roots with the Egyptian Book of the Dead. Egyptians believed that, after their death, they faced a trial in the underworld before Osiris and his forty-two judges in the Hall of Judgment. Spell 125 of this book contains a Negative Confession that the dead person has to recite on this occasion, containing such assurances:

> *I have done no falsehood,*
> *I have not robbed,*
> *I have not stolen,*
> *I have not killed men,*
> *I have not told lies.*

The Ten Commandments are a kind of imperative form of this Egyptian Negative Confession.

> *Thou shalt not kill,*
> *Thou shalt not steal*
> *Thou shalt not bear false witness against thy neighbor.*

It therefore seems that Akhenaten, who did not believe in Osiris and his underworld, turned the moral code according to which the Egyptians believed their dead would be judged into an imperative code of behavior for Aten's followers in this life.

THE DEATH OF MOSES

All through the Old Testament books it can be sensed that there has been a cover-up, an attempt to hide the evidence of a crime for which some Israelite leaders were responsible. Ernest Sellin, the German biblical scholar, who was able to find indications that an important Israelite leader was killed in the wilderness during the time of the Exodus, suggested that the victim was Moses himself, who was murdered by his own followers. He went on to say that despite the efforts of the priests to suppress the sordid story, it nevertheless lived on in prophetic circles.

That an Israelite leader was killed in Sinai—an event Sellin has described as "the scarlet thread" running through Israelite history—is not a new idea. The identity of the victim has been obscured, however, by an elaborate attempt to hide the true facts. This is particularly clear from a chapter in the Book of Numbers, which was largely responsible for persuading Sellin that the assassination took place during the time of the Exodus from Egypt and that Moses himself was the victim. However, although Sellin was right in identifying the actual crime committed in the wilderness of Sinai, he was mistaken about the identity of the victim, as I believe Moses was killed later by Seti I.

The Old Testament account of Moses's failure to reach the Promised Land, his death, and his burial in an unmarked grave is a strange episode. When the Israelites arrived at the area of "the water of Meribah" in the north-central region of Sinai, the Israelites complained of thirst. Moses then used his miraculous rod to smite a rock and bring forth water. Later, according to the Book of Deuteronomy, Moses was punished for this action by being denied the opportunity to enter the Promised Land, no matter how hard he pleaded. Deuteronomy gives the account of Moses's death as such: the Lord asked him to climb up Mount Nebo, in the land of Moab between Sinai and eastern Jordan, and die on the mountain. Then, after admonishing and blessing his people, Moses left them with Joshua and climbed the mountain. There he met his death and was buried by the Lord in an unmarked grave in the plains of Moab below the mount.

In contrast to this story, however, Talmudic sources have a rich collection of contradictory accounts of the manner of Moses's death, which could represent the historical event. A reference to a confrontation between him and the Angel of Death on Mount Nebo before he died, with an indication of a struggle between the two, has persuaded some biblical scholars that Moses was actually killed.

According to the Book of Exodus, the reason is that Moses struck a rock with his rod to obtain water for his thirsty followers. Why should this ordinary action to get water for his followers be the cause of God's punishment? Only when we examine Egyptian sources do we find the real reason for Moses's death and find out who killed him.

When we examine the war record of Seti I, the second king of the Nineteenth Dynasty, we find that his first war was against some nomadic Bedouin tribes in Sinai, named Shasu. "Shasu" is the Egyptian name for the biblical Midianites, who were allied to Moses. They were a nomadic people who spoke a west-Semitic language, and joined Moses in his attempt to leave Egypt for Canaan. The fighting took place in the vicinity of one of the Egyptian fortresses along the military road between the border cities of Zarw and Canaan, which have water wells dug by the army. It would therefore seem to be a more likely explanation—even if it can be only supposition—that Moses, under pressure from his thirsty followers, entered one of these fortresses and obtained water by using his royal scepter. Instructions of this type would have been reported by the Egyptian guards to their superiors at the border city of Zarw, resulting in Seti I sallying forth to put a stop to the unrest in Sinai and, if the Talmudic references to the death of Moses were to be believed, it must have been there that Moses died, out of the sight of his followers.

Fig. 10.4. Seti I returning to Zarw from his war with the Semitic Bedouins in northern Sinai. Photo from the Karnak Temple.

REBELLION IN SINAI

When Ramses I, the founder of the Nineteenth Dynasty, came to the throne toward the end of the fourteenth century BCE, he was already a very old man who did not survive the end of his second year on the throne and was succeeded by his son, Seti I. As soon as Seti came to power, a messenger arrived from Sinai with some disturbing news: The Shasu enemies are plotting rebellion. Their tribal leaders are gathering in one place, standing on the foothills of Khor (the Levant), and they are engaged in turmoil and uproar. Each of them is killing his fellow. They do not consider the laws of the palace.

This campaign took place immediately after the death of Ramses I, even before the process of his mummification, which took seventy days, had been completed and before Seti I had been officially crowned as the new Pharaoh. The full account of Seti I's campaign against the Shasu is found in this king's war reliefs, which occupy the entire exterior of the northern wall of the great Hypostyle Hall in Amun's temple at Karnak. The extreme point in the king's war against the rebels, shown on the bottom row of the eastern side of the wall, is the capture of the city of Pe-Kanan (Gaza). Seti I stopped the rebels leaving Sinai, massacred many, and took many more to be slaughtered at the foot of the Amun image at Karnak.

It was then, most probably, that Seti I killed Moses/Akhenaten, the leader of the rebels, which would also explain how a new version of the Osiris-Set myth came into existence from the time of the Nineteenth Dynasty. Osiris, the king of Egypt, was said to have had to leave the country for a long time. On his eventual return he was assassinated by Set, who had usurped the throne. According to my interpretation of events, it was in fact Set or Seti I who killed Moses at the borders of Sinai.

AKHENATEN'S DEATH

There is no evidence to show that Akhenaten died at the end of his reign in his Year 17, as his royal tomb in Amarna shows that he was not buried there. John Pendlebury, the British archaeologist who excavated the royal tomb at Amarna during the 1930s, found no remains of any of the usual shrine or canopy that were part of the normal burial furniture found in Akhenaten's tomb. What reinforces this conclusion is the fact that, although the evidence indicates that Akhenaten's enemies smashed everything they found in his tomb, no matter how large or small, no part of the main burial furniture has been found. Pendlebury noticed that the canopic chest, which holds the cases containing the internal organs removed during mummification, gives evidence of never having been used, for it is quite unstained by the black resinous substance seen in those of Amenhotep II and Tutankhamun. As the burial rituals required some parts of the funerary furniture, including the canopic chest, to be anointed by a black liquid, and he was unable to see any traces of such staining on the fragments he found, he concluded that the tomb had never been used. Nevertheless, although most Egyptologists accepted the conclusion that Akhenaten could not have been buried in his Amarna tomb, they still believed that he died in his Year 17 and went on looking for his remains in another tomb.

TOMB KV55

The last attempt to claim that Akhenaten's remains have been found was made by Zahi Hawass, the ex-Minister of Egypt's SCA. Hawass rejected my argument about Akhenaten and Moses, refusing to accept that Akhenaten had mixed Egyptian-Israelite blood, which for him was a taboo. When I reminded him that, like Moses, Akhenaten's body has not been found, Hawass decided to prove me wrong by finding the mummy of Akhenaten.

In January 1907 a small tomb—known as Tomb KV55—was found in the Valley of the Kings. The excavation was sponsored by Theodore M. Davis, a rich retired American lawyer and amateur archaeologist, who employed the British archaeologist Edward R. Ayrton to conduct the digs. This tomb, which was used during the reign of Tutankhamun, is located near the entry of the inner Valley of the Kings, close to the site where the tomb of Tutankhamun was subsequently found. It consists of a small, rock-cut chamber approached by a sloping passage and does not seem to have been intended originally for a royal burial. The burial appears to have been carried out in haste, with a minimum of equipment. What made it difficult to establish ownership of the tomb was the fact that it had deteriorated as a result of a great deal of rainwater dripping into it through a fissure in the rock. Inside the tomb the remains of a large wooden gilded shrine were found with inscriptions indicating that it was dedicated by Akhenaten to the burial of his mother, Queen Tiye. A coffin was found in another part of the chamber with inscriptions including the titles and cartouches of Akhenaten and, nearby, there were four canopic jars. Four "magic bricks" to protect the deceased in the underworld were also found in situ, inscribed with the name of Akhenaten. The coffin was originally made for a woman, but adapted for a male burial by the addition of a beard and the alteration of the inscriptions. The face on the coffin had been broken off and the royal names on it—which would have perhaps identified its occupant—had been removed. The coffin had originally lain upon a bier, but, when the wood had eventually rotted away because of the damp, it collapsed and the mummy partly projected from under the lid. The flesh of the mummy had consequently also rotted away leaving the skeleton as the only bodily remains. When the mummy was first discovered, Davis thought it was of Queen Tiye, the mother of king Akhenaten. But later he was disappointed when the remains were examined by Grafton Elliot Smith, Professor of Anatomy in Cairo Medical School, who concluded that the skeleton was that of a man. However, the debate about the identity of the owner of the skeletal mummy in Tomb KV55 has continued up to the present time: is it actually Akhenaten or his brother and son-in-law, Semenkhkare?

The debate about the ownership of tomb KV55 has rumbled on for a whole century, and is still going on. It was Cyril Aldred, the Scottish Egyptologist, who insisted that the skeletal remains of KV55 belonged to Akhenaten. Aldred came to this conclusion because he believed that Akhenaten had peculiar physical characteristics as a result of suffering from a disorder known as "Frohlich's Syndrome," which slows down physical development. He relied on an apparently nude statue of

Akhenaten at Karnak—one of four colossi—which showed the king seemingly deformed and without genitalia (to elaborate a "pathological examination" to discover what disease the king might have suffered from). At the end of the day this proved to be something of a tempest in a tea cup when, however, it was demonstrated eventually that the seemingly nude colossus at Karnak was actually an unfinished statue awaiting the kilt that was seen on the other adjacent three colossi.

The age of skeletal remains in KV55 was the key to the mystery. Since its discovery, almost all examinations of the skeleton showed that it belonged to a young man in his early twenties. Indeed, Grafton Eliot Smith, who first examined the mummy, concluded that the remains belonged to a man of about twenty-five. Another examination was carried out by D. E. Derry, Professor of Anatomy in the Faculty of Medicine at Cairo University. Derry, whose examination included restoring the skull, reported that 1) the conformation of the skull does not support the (Aldred's) conclusion that the person to whom it belonged suffered from hydrocephalus, but to a type known to anthropologists as platycephalic in which the skull is flattened from above downward and correspondingly widened—the reverse of the shape produced by hydrocephalus, and 2) that these remains were those of a man no more than twenty-four years of age. Derry also noticed a similarity between the skull in tomb KV55 and that of Tutankhamun. A third examination in 1963 under the supervision of R. G. Harrison (the late Derby professor of anatomy at the University of Liverpool) confirmed that the skeleton belonged to a man whose death occurred in his twenties. Harrison also confirmed Derry's view of the similarity in facial appearance with Tutankhamun, and concluded that he found no evidence of abnormality.

A fourth examination of tomb KV55's skeletal remains was conducted in 2002 by Joyce M. Filer, British Museum Egyptologist and anthropologist. According to the report, which was published by the *American Journal of Archaeology* in March 2002, Filer's conclusion was categorical and clear.

> The human remains from Tomb 55, as presented to me, are those
> of a young man who had no apparent abnormalities and who was

no older than his early twenties at death and probably a few years younger. If those wanting to identify the remains with Akhenaten demand an age at death of more than mid-twenties, then this is not the man for them.[2] Contrary to all these examinations, Zahi Hawass, claimed that CT scans suggested that the mummy in tomb KV55 belonging to Akhenaten.

Our team was able to establish with a probability of *better than 99.99* percent that Amenhotep III was the father of the individual in KV55, who was in turn the father of Tutankhamun. . . . But *not all the evidence* pointed to Akhenaten. Most forensic analyses had concluded that the body inside was that of a man no older than 25—too young to be Akhenaten—who seems to have sired two daughters before beginning his 17-year reign. Most scholars thus suspected the mummy was instead the shadowy pharaoh Smenkhkare. New CT scans of the KV55 mummy also revealed an age-related degeneration in the spine and osteoarthritis in the knees and legs. It appeared that he had died closer to the age of 40 than 25, as originally thought. With the age discrepancy thus resolved, we could conclude that the KV55 mummy, the son of Amenhotep III and Tiye and the father of Tutankhamun, is almost certainly Akhenaten (Since we know so little about Smenkhkare, *he cannot be completely ruled out.*)[3]

While Hawass started by claiming that his team was able to establish with a probability of better than 99.99 percent that the remains in tomb KV55 belonged to Akhenaten, he finally contradicts himself by concluding that "not all the evidence pointed to Akhenaten" and, "Semenkhkare . . . cannot be completely ruled out." Furthermore, and as at least four medical examinations by prominent international medical experts showed, the mummy in question had a wisdom tooth that was just breaking in, thus strongly indicating a young individual of no more than twenty-five years; therefore, Hawass's conclusion cannot be accepted seriously. Akhenaten is known to have come to the throne at the age of sixteen and ruled for seventeen years, so he could not have been less than thirty-three at the time of death.

In 1931 the golden base of a sarcophagus found in KV55, which had collapsed due to the dampness, disappeared from the Cairo Museum, which, since the discovery of the tomb, has been exhibited in the Cairo Museum under the name of "Semenkhkare." Fifty years later, in 1980, Dr. Dietrich Wildung, Director of the Egyptian Museum in Munich, discovered the "disappeared" base of the sarcophagus, apparently left in the Munich museum by its "owner," a Swiss antique collector who casually had brought it in for restoration! The deteriorated base had some golden sheets with hieroglyphic inscriptions as well as some colored semiprecious stones attached to wood that had much deteriorated. The Munich museum spent more than 200,000 marks in restoration and therefore was not in favor of returning the base of the sarcophagus to Egypt. However, when the Prime Minster of Bavaria visited Cairo on May 3, 2001, he agreed to its return to its home country. When Egypt received the base of Semenkhkare's sarcophagus on January 27, 2002, after seventy-one years of being "lost," Hawass announced this base to belong the sarcophagus of Akhenaten not Semenkhkare. Not surprisingly, Ali Radwan, Professor of Egyptology at Cairo University, rejected outright this identification, saying it was "not correct."

As no respected Egyptologist would accept Hawass's claim of finding his mummy, like Moses, Akhenaten's body must have been buried in an unmarked ditch at the borders of Sinai.

THE EXODUS IN EGYPTIAN SOURCES

At the center of the Bible account there is the story of a Semitic Hebrew tribe descending on Egypt at the time of Joseph, then going back to Canaan some time later, under the leadership of Moses. Biblical scholars and Egyptologists had, up to the mid-twentieth century, regarded the biblical Exodus narration as representing a true historical account. Following the Second World War, however, the situation changed completely. Thanks to archaeological excavations, more light was thrown on the ancient history of both Egypt and Canaan, and the hopes of finding confirmation of the biblical story evaporated. Having excavated all Egyptian locations in the eastern Nile Delta, no evidence was found to support the Exodus account in the Bible.

The lack of archaeological evidence, in my view, was mainly due to the fact that scholars had so far been looking either for evidence to confirm the miraculous accounts in the Bible, such as the parting of the sea, which cannot historically be confirmed, or in the wrong historical period and wrong geographical sites. As they followed biblical chronology, which states that the length of the Israelites' dwelling in Egypt, from their arrival at the time of Joseph to their Exodus with Moses, was 430 years, misled them to search in the wrong locations. In order to allow for the 430 years, they had to date Joseph to the very early period of the Hyksos rule and to fix the Exodus at the last year of Ramses II. Thus both the time of the Descent and the Exodus were decided, not on historical or archaeological evidence, but according to biblical chronology. While looking for Joseph under the Hyksos produced no evidence, searching for the Exodus in the time of Ramses II failed to find any positive result.

Chronology is the backbone of history, and Bible chronology, as we have seen before, provides us with two contradicting dates: 400 years and four generations (which would come to about 100 years). To get out of this uncertainty, it would be better to look for the

Fig. 10.5. Ramses II at Abu Simbel. Photo courtesy of Ahmed Osman.

main biblical characters and major events in Egyptian history, without limiting ourselves to the frame of biblical dates. As both Joseph and Moses were connected to the pharaonic royal house, it should be possible to find them mentioned in Egyptian sources. The situation changes dramatically when we start looking in Egyptian sources for evidence of the Israelite Exodus. To start with, the Israel Stele, the only archaeological evidence in Egypt that mentions Israel by name, confirms that the Israelites were already in Canaan in the fifth year of Merenptah's rule, who succeeded Ramses II during the last quarter of the thirteenth century BCE. This evidence indicates clearly that the Israelites must have left Egypt at a considerable time before that date, to allow for their forty years of wandering in Sinai and their settlement in Canaan.

When we look for evidence of Israelites living in Egypt before their Exodus, we find significant archaeological discovery in Saqqara. In 1987 Alain-Pierre Zivie, the French archaeologist, discovered the tomb of Aper-el who was a vizier of both Amenhotep III and Akhenaten during the time of their coregency. Aper-el's or Aperel's name indicates that he was of a Hebrew origin, related to Israelite God El or Elohim. Aperel's tomb was discovered at the cliffs of the Bubasteion, a sanctuary dedicated to the cat deity Bastet, at the necropolis of Memphis in Saqqara. He also seems to have been related to Yuya, whom he succeeded as a commander of the chariots, and is believed to have been between fifty and sixty years old at the time of his death. As the discovery of Aperel's tomb has raised many questions regarding the connection between this vizier and the presence of the Israelites in Egypt, Zahi Hawass, the ex-minister of the SCA, tried to undermine the significance of this discovery.

> In my opinion, the Israelite Exodus from Egypt will remain a point of controversy among scientists and researchers until the Day of Judgment or until new archaeological evidence is unearthed that is able to settle this issue. However, in the light of the information currently available to historians and archaeologists, we can do no more than practice moderation and caution. There have been

whispers in the archaeological community following the discovery of the Aper-el tomb in the Saqqara region in the area known as Abwab al-Qotat (Doors of the Cats) by French archaeologist Alain Zivie. Abwab al-Qotat was given its name following the discovery of thousands of mummified cats interred in the tombs. . . . The discovery of this tomb, which took place almost twenty years ago, remains an important archaeological event. The reason for this is that the person buried in the tomb was known as "Aper-el" and this is an Egyptianized form of a Hebrew name. Aper-el was the vizier of King Amenhotep III, and later his son King Akhenaten. Pharaoh Akhenaten was the first ruler to institute monotheism represented by the worship of the sun, which he called Aten.

Excavations of this tomb continued for almost ten years, beginning in 1980 and ending in late 1989. Amongst the artefacts discovered here were several portraits titled "spiritual father of Aten" as well as "the Priest" and "the first servant of Aten." This means that Aper-el served as the chief priest of Aten in the Memphis region during the reign of King Akhenaten. Of course the effects of the news of the discovery of a Hebrew tomb have raised many questions and controversies among archaeologists with regards to whether or not a temple for Aten existed in Memphis. The portraits found in the Aper-el tomb indicate that such a temple did, in fact, exist in Memphis, and this is contrary to the tradition accepted by archaeologists, which is that monotheism (Atenism) did not exist beyond the city of Tell el-Amarna in central Egypt. Tell-Amarna was the city founded by Akhenaten for his family. Akhenaten swore never to depart the city so long as he lived, and he named it Akhet-Aten meaning the city faithful and loyal to Aten.

In addition to this, there has been prolonged controversy between Torah scholars and archaeologists over the credibility of Aper-el in fact being a Hebrew name. This creates the impression that Hebrews were present in Egypt during the Eighteenth Dynasty, and that some Egyptianized Hebrews held senior state positions. It is important to emphasize that all the artefacts discovered in the Aper-el tomb, such as the sarcophagus, the mummies, as well as the carvings on the walls of the tomb, are consistent with the Egyptian style of the time. Even Aper-el's portrait, his clothes, and his jewelry are purely ancient Egyptian.[4]

In his report on the tomb, Zivie said

The decoration on the main central niche remained in a very good state of preservation. On the sides are paintings of the vizier, each with his complete name, Aper-El, receiving offerings of flowers from two sons previously unknown to us. Their names and titles are present: one, Seny, was a high official; the other, Hataiy, was a priest. The representations are important because they illustrate the art of the time of Akhenaten (the Amarna Period) and its aftermath not at Amarna or at Thebes, but rather at Memphis, which remained the main city of the country.[5]

Here we find a strong archaeological evidence to show that around year 1360 BCE, during the time of the Eighteenth Dynasty, about a century and a quarter before the death of Ramses II, an Israelite Hebrew was serving as a vizier, the highest official office in the country after Pharaoh. Not only was Aper-el a follower of Akhenaten who became the Priest of his monotheistic God Aten in Memphis, he could also have been related to the Egyptian king. The fact that Queen Tiye was associated with her husband in donating a box to the funerary furniture of Aper-el indicates the possibility that the vizier was a relation of the queen's and her son, through her Israelite father, Yuya/Joseph.

If we again were to ignore the chronology of the Bible and start looking for evidence of an exodus of Semitic Bedouin groups out of Egyptian Sinai and into Canaan, then the situation also changes dramatically, and we soon find evidence for the one and only such attempt, which took place at the end of Ramses I's short reign.

Pa-Ramses, who later became Ramses I and established the Nineteenth Dynasty, was one of the five generals who forced Akhenaten to abdicate the throne and go to exile in Sinai. After the disappearance of Aye, the last of the Amarna kings, who was also Akhenaten's maternal uncle, Horemheb married Nefertiti's sister, Mutnezmat, to gain the right to the throne. As he had no children, Horemheb appointed Pa-Ramses to be his heir, as well as being the vizier and commander of his army. Because he was a local resident at the border city of Zarw, Ramses was also appointed as the governor of this fortified border city, which supervised the whole border area of northern Sinai, including the land of Goshen and which Horemheb had turned into a prison for Akhenaten's followers. Ramses himself belonged to a local family coming from the area of Zarw, and it is this Ramses who must have been remembered by the Hebrew scribes putting down the biblical account.

At the time of his accession, Ramses I was already a very old man and did not survive the end of his second year on the throne. At the same time, it has been confirmed that his death coincided with a rebellion of some Semitic groups in Sinai who were attempting to cross the Egyptian borders into Canaan. Immediately after the death of Ramses I (ca. 1333 BCE) we find evidence of some Semitic Bedouin tribes of Sinai, called Shasu by the Egyptians, attempting to cross the Egyptian borders to Canaan.

On the east side of the northern wall of the great Hypostyle Hall in Amun's temple at Karnak, we find two series of scenes distributed symmetrically on either side of the entrance to the temple representing the wars of Seti I, the second king of the Nineteenth Dynasty who succeeded his father Ramses I on the throne. The first of these wars chronologically is found at the bottom row of the east wall; it is the war against the Shasu. The rhetorical texts claim that Pharaoh received a report that the Shasu-Bedouin are plotting rebellion, as discussed in the section, "Rebellion in Sinai" (see page 121).

SHASU AND MIDIANITES

The Shasu, mentioned only in Egyptian texts, were seminomadic Bedouins who lived in tents and raised cattle. Shasu was the name given by the Egyptians to this group, who are known in both the Bible and the Qu'ran as the Midianites. They were allies of Moses, and it seems that they were part of the Semitic groups who attempted to leave Egypt into Canaan at the Exodus. During the reign of Amenhotep II (1436–1413 BCE), the son of Thutmose III established the Egyptian Empire. It was reported that he captured some Apiru nomads and a large number of Shasu, who dwelled in Sinai as well as southern Palestine.

Later during the time of his grandson Amenhotep III, a topographical list inscribed on his temple at Soleb in Nubia mentions a number of cities and regions conquered during his reign, including six "lands of the Shasu," referring to nomadic people associated with Sinai, the Negev in southern Canaan, as well as Transjordan. One of the lands mentioned on the Soleb list of Amenhotep III is *sr'r* with a probable reading of Seir (an ancient reference of Edom), which would read "Shusu of Seir." Even more interesting in the Soleb list is the reading *t3 shsw yhw* ("Yahweh in the land of the Shasu") as a result of which Raphael Giveon, the Egyptologist at Tel Aviv University, suggested that the toponym *Yhw* is the Tetragrammaton of the God of Israel.[6] This agrees with the biblical references to Israel's contact with people from Midian, who knew the name of Yahweh (Exodus 3:1; 18:1, 10–11). Many scholars do accept this connection, which may show a worship of Yahweh and contact between Israel and Midian at an early period. It would also include Midianites under the broad Egyptian term "Shasu" as Bedouin if they can be associated with "Yahweh in the land of the Shasu."

Meanwhile, in 1967, Raphael Patai, a Hungarian-Jewish historian, suggested that Yahweh had a wife called Asherah who was worshipped together with him. His theory gained new prominence due to the research of Francesca Stavrakopoulou, senior lecturer in the Department of Theology at the University of Exeter, who declared, "After years of research specializing in the history and religion of Israel . . . I have come to a colorful and what could seem to some, uncomfortable conclusion that God had a wife."[7] Asherah's connection to Yahweh, according to Stavrakopoulou, is spelled out in both the Bible and an eighth-century BCE inscription on pottery found in the northeast Sinai desert at a site called "Kuntillet Ajrud," a fortress on the road between Egypt and Canaan. The inscription, a petition for a blessing, asks for a blessing from "Yahweh and his Asherah." Stavrakopoulou also points out that Asherah was worshipped in Yahweh Temple in Jerusalem, and the Book

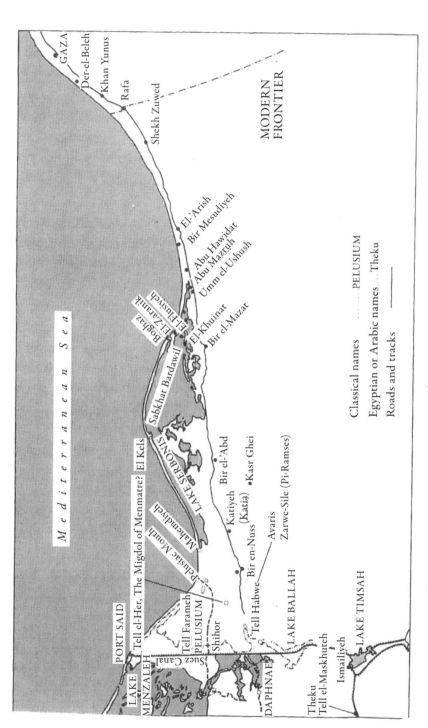

Fig. 10.6. The Horus Road, between Zarw and Gaza.

of Kings reports that a statue of Asherah was housed in the temple and that female temple personnel vowed ritual textiles to her. J. Edward Wright, President of both The Arizona Center for Judaic Studies and The Albright Institute for Archaeological Research, told *Discovery News* that he agrees that several Hebrew inscriptions mention Yahweh and his Asherah. Asherah and Ashtarot, known across the ancient Near East by various names, such as Astarte and Ishtar, was an important deity whose name has been translated in the English Bible as "Sacred Tree."

Going back to the rebellion in Sinai, as soon as he received the disturbing news, even before having being able to bury his father, Seti led his army out of the border city of Zarw along the route in northern Sinia called "the Ways of Horus" by the Egyptians and known in the Bible as "the way of the land of the Philistines." The route consisted of a series of military forts, each with a well, that are depicted in detail in the king's war scenes at Karnak. The king carried on pushing along the road in the Negeb, scattering the Shasu, who from time to time gathered in sufficient numbers to meet him. One of these actions is depicted in the Karnak relief as taking place on the desert road. Over the battle scene stands the inscription: "The Good God, Sun of Egypt, Moon of all land, Montu in the foreign countries . . . like Baal . . . The rebels, they know not how they shall (flee); the vanquished of the Shasu (becoming like) that which existed not."

Seti continued on his way into Edom, south of the Dead Sea, and the land of Moab in modern Jordan before returning to the northern Sinai road between Zarw and Gaza until he reached Canaan itself. Just across the Egyptian border he arrived at a fortified town whose name is given as Pe-Kanan, which is believed to be the city of Gaza. Another scene has the following inscription over the defeated Shasu.

Year 1, King of Upper and Lower Egypt, Menma-re. The destruction, which the mighty sword of Pharaoh made among the vanquished of the Shasu from the fortress of Zarw to Pe-Kanan, when His Majesty marched against them like a fierce-eyed lion, making them carcasses in their valleys, overturned in their blood like those that exist not.

After fighting a running battle with the Shasu Bedouin, who were never a serious threat to Pharaoh's army, Seti arrived in Gaza and began the main part of his campaign of Year 1 progressing north through Canaan all the way into Lebanon. When he returned victoriously to Zarw, Seti traveled to Thebes in Upper Egypt, where a big celebration took place at Amun's Karnak temple, and where Pharaoh sacrificed some of his Shasu prisoners at the feet of Amun's image. There are scenes devoted to the presentation of booty to the god Amun-Re. The caption over one reads:

> Presentation of tribute by His Majesty to his father Amun. . . consisting of silver, gold, lapis-lazuli, turquoise, red jasper and every sort of precious stone. The chiefs of the hill country are in his grasp to fill the workshops of his father Amun.

Thus Seti I prevented the Exodus of the Semites into Canaan, and they had to go back to living in Sinai for many years before they were able to infiltrate into East Jordan, which completely agrees with the biblical account of the Exodus. For according to chapter 14 of the Book of Numbers, the Israelites were not able to enter the Promised Land before wandering in Sinai for forty years. Following the miraculous crossing of the Red Sea, the Israelites spent eleven months at Mount Sinai, and soon began to complain about their hardship. The Israelites complained about the food, and their complaining angered God and frustrated Moses. They also grumbled against Moses and wanted to return back to Egypt, and talked about stoning Moses and Aaron. So God punished them by forbidding all this generation from entering the Promised Land. They will all die in the Sinai desert, as only their children will be allowed in forty years.

We also have textual reports that the Shasu rebels were able to leave Sinai some years later during the reign of Seti's successor, Ramses II (ca. 1304–1237 BCE), and their number in Transjordan was reported to have increased significantly. It was then that the first real explicit reference to Moab and Seir appears in Egyptian texts. Ramses II described himself as one "who plunders the mountain of Seir with his valiant

Fig. 10.7. Ramses II making an offering. A handout picture released by Egypt's Supreme Council of Antiquities on April 21, 2009, shows carving on a wall at an ancient temple in the Sinai Peninsula.

arm" with parallel mentions to Shasu in context. Ramses II is known to have campaigned in Transjordan, including in Moab and Seir, and obviously considered it significant enough to raid or conquer this territory, and the first reference to "Edom" as an entity (as opposed to the more ancient "Seir"), along with clear mentions of the Shasu coming from that region, comes from the time of Ramses II's son and successor Merenptah around 1206 BCE. A passage from Papyrus Anastasi VI reports an event that took place in the eighth year of Merenptah.

> We have finished with allowing the Shasu clans folk of Edom to pass the fort of Merenptah that is in Succoth in the land of Goshen, to the pools of Pi-Atum of Merenptah that are in Succoth, to keep them alive and to keep alive their livestock.[8]

This shows a more normal relationship between Egyptians and the Shasu Bedouin, who were coming down to Egypt from Edom, to find water and pasture for their flocks during some difficult circumstances.

Away from biblical chronology, we have the evidence of the Israelite Exodus from Egypt, confirmed by Egyptian archaeology, which makes Horemheb the Pharaoh of Oppression and Ramses I the Pharaoh of the Exodus.

11

THE SEMITIC PHARAOH
OF THE EXODUS

The mummy of Pharaoh Ramses I, which had been lost for more than 140 years, was found a few years ago in a small American museum, and was returned to Egypt on October 26, 2003. The Atlanta Michael Carlos Museum gave it back when tests showed that it belonged to the Pharaoh who established the Nineteenth Dynasty of ancient Egypt. Michael Carlos Museum acquired the mummy in 1999 from a Canadian museum, which had bought it from a private collector in 1860 who smuggled it from Luxor. When it reached Egypt, Ramses' body was carried off the plane in a box draped in the national flag, on its way to the Cairo Museum.

The body is remarkably well-preserved, filled with resin and stuffed with rolled linen some thirty-three centuries ago. The mummy showed that Ramses was about five feet five inches tall, balding, and has a mouthful of teeth and an intact facial profile. His arms crossed over the chest right over left, as was typical for Pharaohs of the era, while his left hand looks as if it had grasped an object, possibly a scepter, and his toes separated by gold plates, a ceremony reserved for royalty.

Enough evidence was found to indicate this unnamed mummy was the remains of the missing pharaoh Ramses I. Egyptologists at the

Fig. 11.1. The mummy of Ramses I. Courtesy of the Museum of Atlanta, Georgia.

Atlanta Michael Carlos Museum in Atlanta, Georgia, were able to identify him among nine mummies that were brought in a few years before from the Niagara Falls Daredevil Museum in Canada. Radiocarbon-dating roughly placed the mummy's origin in the time when Ramses I ruled Egypt. Together with other circumstantial evidence—the location of the tomb that was looted, the style in which the mummy was wrapped and embalmed, and its facial features—helped to establish the mummy's identity. X-rays of the mummies showed this one bore a striking resemblance to the Ramesside rulers of the Nineteenth Dynasty, and DNA tests on his teeth matched him with the mummies of his children in the Cairo Museum.

When examining his facial appearance, it became clear that the features of Ramses I, the Pharaoh who oppressed the Semitic tribes of Israel, proved to be Semitic himself. Like all the Ramesside kings who ruled Egypt after him for 150 years, Ramses I had strong Semitic features with a large fleshy nose known as the "Ra hook-nose." Perhaps most compelling is a facial profile that is strikingly similar to the mummy of his grandson Ramses II, a great builder and warrior, as well as Yuya, Queen Tiye's father. However, when we know that Ramses originated at the very location of the Semitic Hyksos rulers of Avaris, it becomes less surprising.

Ramses I was born to a noble military family during the reign of Amenhotep III, at the border city of Zarw, which had been established in the same location as Avaris. The son of a local troop commander called Seti, Ramses did not have royal blood. Both General Pa-Ramses and his son, General Seti I, were appointed by Horemheb as mayors of the city of Zarw and commanders of its fortress.

> Now there came the Hereditary Prince; Mayor of the City and Vizier; Fan-Bearer on the Right Hand of the King, Troop Commander; Overseer of Foreign Countries; Overseer of the Fortress of Sile (Zarw); . . . Seti I, the triumphant, the son of the Hereditary Prince (Pa-Ramses); Mayor of the City and Vizier; Troops Commander; Overseer of Foreign Countries; Overseer of the Fortress of Sile; Royal Scribe; and Master of Horse . . .[1]

But when the childless Pharaoh Horemheb, the last of the Eighteenth Dynasty rulers, fell mortally ill, Pa-Ramses was the logical strongman to succeed him. Nevertheless, his rule lasted for less than two years, believed to be either 1292 to 1290 or 1295 to 1294 BCE. Before ascending the throne, he also served as the high priest of Amun and as such, he would have played an important role in the restoration of the old religion following the Amarna religious revolution under Akhenaten. The fact that he was born in the city of Zarw, the same location as the previous Avaris of the Hyksos, makes it more likely that he was a descendent of the Hyksos family. This, however, does not mean that the Ramessides were of non-Egyptian origin.

RAMSES II WORSHIPS OF SETH-SETI

Another connection between the Ramesside kings and the Hyksos comes from the similarity of their religious beliefs. Like the Hyksos, Ramses I and his successors worshipped Seth, whose name was worn by both his father and his son. Seth had been associated with the area of the eastern delta at the frontier, near the start of Sinai desert and the road to Asia. It is even thought that the whole of the fourteenth nome, the northeastern area of the delta between the ancient Pelusiac branch of the Nile and Kantarah at the Suez Canal, was named Stheroite after this deity. From the end of the Sixth Dynasty, during the twenty-second century BCE, Seth had been discredited as a result of the development of the myth that he had been responsible for the assassination of the good god Osiris: he became associated with evil and is the source of the later name Satan. However, at the very start of the Hyksos takeover, Nehesy, a ruler of the weak Thirteenth Dynasty, reestablished the worship of "Seth, Lord of Avaris" as the chief deity of the fourteenth nome. According to Manfred Bietak, the Austrian Egyptologist:

> Nehesy (ca. 1715 BCE) is known from several monuments as the first king with the title "Beloved of Seth, Lord of Avaris." This Seth later became the principal god of the Hyksos, but was clearly established in Avaris by the local dynasty before the rise of the Hyksos rule.[2]

Further confirmation of this is provided by the 400-year stele, the most important evidence regarding the continuity of worship of the god Seth at Avaris for four centuries. Although the stele was actually found at Tanis, which became the new capital toward the end of the Twenty-first Dynasty; it was not in situ, and it must have been moved there from Zarw. The stele was erected by Ramses II in honor of his father Seti I whose family came from the city of Avaris, former fortress of the Hyksos. As well as being the main god of the Hyksos, Seth was considered the ancestor of the Ramessides. The stele refers to the commemoration of a 400-year anniversary relating to the worship of Seth in Avaris, which had also been performed by Ramses II's father Seti I, while he was still a Commander of the army under Horemheb. The scene at the top shows Ramses II offering wine to the god Seth in his Asiatic form used in Sinai, accompanied by his father Seti, son of Pa-Ramses, when he was then the vizier of Horemheb and the mayor of the fortress of Zarw. The inscription says that His Majesty has commanded to raise a great stele in granite, for the name of his father's Seti I and Ramses I.

The celebration of Seth's worship at Zarw is a further pointer to the fortified city having occupied the same site as Pi-Ramses and Avaris, and the fact that both these high officials of Horemheb, who became the first two kings of the Nineteenth Dynasty, had all their titles relating them to Zarw and to nowhere else is a further implication that they

must have had a residence at Zarw during their vizierates. It is this residence that is most likely to have been rebuilt to become what was later
called Pi-Ramses.

HYKSOS FROM SINAI

The prevailing idea that the Hyksos were foreigners who came from
Asia has been challenged recently by Thomas L. Thompson. Although
the origin of the Hyksos had been a subject of disagreement among
scholars who have thought of the identity of the Hyksos as Arabs,
horse-breeders from Asia, Hittites, Indo-Iranians, or Hurrians, the general view now regards them as Canaanites, who migrated to Egypt from
Palestine. Thompson, Professor of Old Testament at the University
of Copenhagen, remarks that "all but few modern scholars have
accepted the conclusion uncritically that the Hyksos were originally
Palestinians."[3]

> In the early years of modern research, scholars identified the Hyksos
> with the kings of the Fifteenth Dynasty of Egypt, who ruled from
> about 1670 to 1570 BCE. The early scholars accepted Manetho's
> report quite literally and sought evidence for a powerful foreign
> nation or ethnic group that came from afar to invade and con-
> quer Egypt. Subsequent studies showed that inscriptions and seals
> bearing the names of Hyksos rulers were West Semitic—in other
> words—Canaanite. Recent archaeological excavations in the east-
> ern Nile Delta have confirmed that conclusion and indicate that
> the Hyksos "invasion" was a gradual process of immigration from
> Canaan to Egypt, rather than a lightning military campaign.
>
> The most important dig has been undertaken by Manfred
> Bietak, of the University of Vienna, at Tell ed-Dab'a, a site in the
> eastern delta identified as Avaris, the Hyksos capital. Excavations
> there show a gradual increase of Canaanite influence in the styles
> of pottery, architecture, and tombs from around 1800 BCE. By the
> time of the Fifteenth Dynasty, some 150 years later, the culture of
> the site, which eventually became a huge city, was overwhelmingly

Canaanite. The Tell ed-Dab'a finds are evidence for a long and gradual development of Canaanite presence in the delta, and a peaceful takeover of power there.[4]

Thompson came to a completely different conclusion, rejecting the view that the Hyksos had come from another country, and regarding them to be native Egyptians who settled in the eastern delta. Accordingly Thomson regards the war of liberation by Ahmose and the princes of Thebes as a conflict between the traditional rulers of Upper Egypt and the new Lower Egyptian rulers of the delta. From the beginning of Egyptian history up to the time of the Hyksos ruler, all ruling families came from Upper Egypt, who believed that they alone had the right to rule. Thompson also rejects the idea that Ahmose I, who came down from Thebes to get rid of the Hyksos rulers, got rid of the Semitic population that had settled in the delta, for all he did was to get rid of their Hyksos rulers and establish his own Upper Egyptian Eighteenth Dynasty.

It is, I believe, surely a mistake to expand the Kamose Stele's reference to the Fifteenth Dynasty's Apophis as a "Prince of Retenu" into a thesis of Hyksos empire in southern Palestine, let alone to see this as supporting an understanding of the so-called Hyksos rule of Egypt as a southern extension of a Palestinian empire! A. Kempinski's suggestion of a Fifteenth-Dynasty Egyptian Empire, centered in southern Palestine and the Delta, in competition for control of the southern Levant with the kingdom of Aleppo in Syria, as an immediate predecessor of the Eighteenth Dynasty's imperial control of Palestine in competition with the Hittites (of Asia Minor) too readily translates linguistic, cultural and trade relationships into direct political and military control. Whatever the significance of the Eighteenth-Dynasty propaganda against its predecessors in Egypt, the West Semitic linguistic connections between Palestine and Egypt hardly needs such an imperial explanation. The Fifteenth Dynasty's base of political power was wholly Egyptian, albeit oriented to the Egyptian delta, and the caricature of some of its rulers as "foreign" hegemony *heka kh3 swt* is little more than a reflex of the Eighteenth Dynasty's Theban proclivity to exclude the Delta's Semites from their understanding of what they felt was truly Egyptian. This "foreign" hegemony of the Fifteenth and Sixteenth Dynasty over Egypt that had reduced "Egypt" to a region sandwiched between the territories of the Asiatic from Avaris in the north to that of the black Africans in the south. . . . This so-called Asiatic domination was overthrown when Thebes reasserted its control over Egypt and drove the "Asiatics" (*'3mw*) from Egypt under Ahmose I.[5]

Thompson's explanation makes it clear that the rule of the eleven Ramesside kings of the Nineteenth and Twentieth Dynasties, who came from the delta, represent the end of the Upper Egyptian rulers. However, in order to understand the reason behind Thompson's conclusions, we have to see how the Egyptian state was formed about twelve centuries before the Hyksos rule, and how Egypt was unified under the authority of Upper Egypt.

DELTA IN PREHISTORY

Agriculture was the turning point in the history of mankind, which prepared the ground for the emergence of modern civilizations. This great step, which took place in the Near East, allowed larger human groups to settle down in villages and towns and establish permanent communities. The next step was the unification of some of these villages and towns in one social community and one political entity, under one ruling authority. This major step in the development of human civilization took place in Egypt: the first country to be unified in one political state. From about 5,200 years ago, Egypt became the only country in the world to form a central political state whose borders extend from Palestine and the Mediterranean in the north, to Nubia and Aswan in the south.

When the ice age came to an end 12,000 years ago huge glaciers on the high African mountains of Ethiopia, Kenya, and Uganda started to melt, sending massive volumes of water down to the north. As the water finally reached Lower Egypt, it caused catastrophic floods, washing away all habitation; the area of the Nile Delta remained threatened by the yearly floods for thousands of years more, suitable neither for human habitation nor for farming. Eventually, by about 2000 BCE, the Nile Delta emerged as a large fertile land in Lower Egypt. About 23 km (about 14 miles) north of Cairo, the Nile divides into two branches that meander gradually through the delta: the western branch reaches the Mediterranean at Rosetta, while the eastern one ends at Damietta.

> The fertile soil of the Delta, comprising clay and silt mixed with sands brought from the volcanic plains of Ethiopia, has produced a region of meadows and cultivated land concentrated in an area of 22,000 square kilometers, which accounts for 63 percent of the habitable surface of the country as a whole. This hunting ground of the pharaohs . . . is a fertile triangle marked in many different ways by the traces of river branches and fossil canals that have been silted up since ancient times.[6]

The history of Egypt began 1,200 years before the Nile Delta became inhabited, when King Narmer (Menes) was able to unify the Two Lands of Egypt and establish the first ruling dynasty. According to later Egyptian tradition, the nation's history began around 3200 BCE with the unification of Upper and Lower Egypt into a single kingdom under the first Pharaoh of the First Dynasty, known as Menes. This situation raises some questions regarding the nature of the Two Lands that were unified by Narmer. It has been thought that the Two Lands represent Upper and Lower Egypt (i.e. the delta). Now, however, this understanding has to be questioned as no evidence of human habitation has been found in most of the delta at the time Narmer unified Egypt. Up to the start of the second millennium BCE, the delta was covered with marshes unsuitable for farming or for residence. It was covered with swamps and could not have represented the land that was unified with Upper Egypt.

By 3100 BCE Egypt had become the first nation-state in the world, unified under the command of divine kings, with all the administrative requirements that this entailed. The success of this new political arrangement depended on their new invention: writing.[7]

As the delta had not yet been inhabited at the time when Narmer unified Egypt about 3200 BCE, what does the expression "Two Lands" represent?

We know that the Sinai Peninsula, located in western Asia, became part of unified Egypt from the very beginning, at the time of Narmer. We also know that Sinai had been inhabited in prehistory for a long time before the time of Narmer. For Sinai was not completely a barren desert; streams of fresh water, springing from clefts in the rock, are found at about 25-kilometer (about 15-mile) intervals. It also has small oases, where date palms grow along the banks of running water. Wheat, barley, and all sorts of trees are cultivated, and there are many trees and rare flowers. Archaeological evidence shows that Upper Egyptians were using the Sinaitic turquoise mines at Serabit el-Khadim, even before the time of Narmer.

While ancient Egyptian texts speak of the unification of the Two Lands in one political state, there has been some misunderstanding in modern times regarding what those two lands represent. When they refer to the unification of Egypt, scholars usually talk about the North and the South, or Lower Egypt and Upper Egypt. This, however, seems to be a misleading statement, as the Egyptians themselves didn't explain their Two Lands in this way. Instead, Egyptian texts referring to the unification always talk about the Black land and the Red land. While the Egyptians called the Nile Valley "black earth" (*kemet*), they referred to the desert as the "red earth" (*ta desharet*), so the union must have taken place between the Nile Valley and the desert, represented by the only inhabited desert of Sinai. The unification of the two lands allowed for a centralization of authority which, as a result, became able to undertake massive administrative and building projects.

This unification, however, seems to have been achieved through some military conquests in the north, as military scenes were carved on a number of palettes dated to the late pre-Dynastic period.

Scenes and signs on the Narmer Mace-head present war captives and booty, and conquered peoples are also represented on the Scorpion Mace-head. Such scenes suggest that warfare played a role at some point in the forming of the early state in Egypt.[8]

The Sinai Peninsula had a prehistory that is vouched for by the many remains of ancient settlements and temples, as well as inscriptions found there. The oldest remains of settlements in North Sinai have been dated to 32,000 BCE and the earliest proof of contact with the Nile Valley dates to 8000 BCE. Some inscriptions show that Sinai was occupied by Upper Egyptian forces at the time of the Egyptian First Dynasty (3200 BCE), while contact with some mines dates even earlier. From the First Dynasty onward, inscriptions by the Pharaohs appeared regularly on the local rocks, recording their conquests and expeditions to the mines and quarries. The earliest of these inscriptions belongs to King Horus-Den of the First Dynasty, who is represented as a defeated Bedouin chieftain.

It is clear that Sinai became part of unified Egypt from the time of Narmer, the first king of the First Dynasty, while the Nile Delta was still covered by swamps. Thus the Two Lands represented the Red land of the Sinai Peninsula, and the Black land of the Nile Valley, whose territory extended from the borders of Canaan in the north to Aswan in the south. As for the nature of Egypt's population, while those who dwell in the Nile Valley were of African origin, the inhabitants of Sinai were of Semitic Arabian origin. It was these Asiatics of Sinai who were called *amu* in Egyptian texts. Later, when around 2000 BCE the Nile Delta became a dry land suitable for cultivation and habitation, the first people to move in were those living next door in Sinai who settled there to cultivate the new rich agricultural land. Although they shared the same racial origin as the Canaanites, they had become Egyptians twelve centuries earlier.

NARMER'S PALETTE

The unification of Egypt is represented by the Narmer Palette, now in the Cairo Museum. This palette, which has a shield shape, was cut out of one piece of dark-green-colored schist, with both sides decorated and carved in raised relief, including the oldest known specimens of hieroglyphic writing. At the top of both sides are the central serekhs bearing the hieroglyphic signs of Narmer's name. The top scene takes up most of the recto of the Narmer Palette, dominated by a large figure of the king with a ceremonial beard and wearing the White Crown of Upper Egypt and a symbolic bull's tail. In his right hand the king wields a mace, ready to smash the skull of a kneeling bearded man, whom he holds by his long hair with his left hand. Above the victim's head in front of Narmer's face, the falcon Horus—symbol of Egyptian royalty and protector of the king—is sitting upon the plants of personified papyrus marshland.

The back of the palette is divided into three levels. Above the top level, the king's name, "Narmer," is written inside a serekh, which is flanked on each side by a cow's head, possibly a reference to the goddess Hathor represented as a cow. Hathor was the patron goddess of miners, who had a great temple on the south Sinai Mount of Serabit el-Khadim, as well as being the protector goddess in the desert regions. On the left-hand side of the top lever, the king is represented wearing the Red Crown of Lower Egypt. In his left hand, he holds a mace, in the other a flail, symbol of his royalty. He is preceded by his vizier, and a female figure holding a scepter in her left hand. All the people are represented smaller than the king. The procession is walking toward ten decapitated bodies—divided into rows of five persons each—lying on the ground with their disembodied heads between their legs. They represent the king's vanquished enemies.

In the central scene, two persons tie together the elongated necks of two feline animals, which could be alluding to panthers, symbol of the eastern and western heavens. In the bottom scene, the Apis bull is represented trampling a scared, naked, bearded foe. The dominant theme, however, is the victory of the god incarnate over the forces of evil and chaos.

Who were Narmer's enemies represented in this palette? Although the palette refers to the marshland of the delta, the vanquished chiefs it depicts do not look like the Lower Egyptians, with their beards and long hair. On the other hand, at the time of Egyptian unification, the Nile Delta was still like a marshland, uninhabited and uncultivated. Except for Buto, modern Tell el-Fra'in, 40 km (25 miles) south of the Mediterranean coast, the delta had no pre-Dynastic settlements. The only pre-Dynastic settlements in Lower Egypt were located either on the southwestern corner of the delta, at Merinda Bani Salama, or to the east of the delta, Minshat Abu Omar, and Tell Ibrahim Awad and Tell el-Iswid. This situation continued for more than 1,000 years, before the delta itself became inhabitable and cultivated. On the other hand, Sinai was part of the unified Two Lands of Egypt from the time of the First Dynasty. The Egyptians mined turquoise in Sinai at two locations, now called by their Arabic names Wadi Maghareh and Serabit el-Khadim. At the same time, Lower Nubia in the south was controlled by the central Egyptian state from the Early Dynastic Period. At this early date, Egypt even controlled the land of Palestine, although this situation did not last long.

> Contact between northern Egypt and Palestine at this time was overland, as evidence in the northern Sinai demonstrates. Between Qantr [Qantara] and Raphia, about 250 early settlements have been located by the North Sinai Expedition of Ben Gurion University. . . . Not only did the Egyptians establish camps and way stations in the northern Sinai, but the ceramic evidence also suggests that they established a highly organized network of settlements in southern Palestine where an Egyptian population was in residence.[9]

At the time of the Old Kingdom from the Third to the Sixth Dynasties of the pyramid builders, Egypt saw a long period of stability and economic prosperity. This period, however, came to an end as a result of long-time famine, which caused the collapse of the central government. The country was divided into provinces as drought and hunger, as well as violence and crime, spread in the land around 2181 BCE. This was followed by a period of disunity and cultural decline that is known as the First Intermediate Period. The Middle Kingdom started from the establishment of the Eleventh Dynasty until the end of the Thirteenth Dynasty, between 2055 and 1650 BCE. Then the central government began to weaken again until it collapsed completely during the Fourteenth Dynasty. Rulers were not able to govern their lands for more than a few months, and so over that 150 years, sixty kings sat on the throne of the Two Lands. At the end, Hyksos rulers took over control of the delta from where they extended their domination all over Egypt.

What persuaded Thompson to reject the idea that the Hyksos came from Canaan is the fact that archaeological excavation in Palestine for the same period has not shown enough human resources to be able to establish control over the delta. Although Palestine evidence indicates the existence of trade relation between Hyksos Egypt with Canaan and Syria, no military or political relation existed. During that period, eighteenth to seventeenth centuries BCE, no central political authority was formed in Canaan, only small scattered villages and towns that would not allow a military force to invade Egypt. As for the Hyksos own cultural elements, they used the same elements of Egyptian civilization in art and writing and, while not leaving much architecture, they worshipped Seth the killer of Osiris.

After a long period of infiltration by Bedouins from Sinai who settled in the eastern delta, which lasted for more than 100 years, the Hyksos rulers imposed their control first on the fortified border city, which they called Avaris, and extended their control over the rest of Egypt during the rule of their Fifteenth to Seventeenth Dynasties, before they were driven out by Ahmose I in the middle of the sixteenth century BCE. Manetho, the Egyptian historian of the third century BCE, mentioned their arrival as such.

> Tutimaeus. In his reign, for what cause I know not, a blast of God smote us; and unexpectedly, *from the regions of the East,* invaders of obscure race marched in confidence of victory against our land. By main force they easily overpowered the rulers of the land, they then burned our cities ruthlessly, razed to the ground the temples of the gods, and treated all the natives with a cruel hostility, massacring some and leading into slavery the wives and children of others.

Finally, they appointed as king one of their number, whose name was Salities. *He had his seat at Memphis,* levying tribute from Upper and Lower Egypt, and always leaving garrisons behind in the most advantageous positions. Above all, *he fortified the district to the east,* foreseeing that the Assyrians, as they grew stronger, would one day covet and attack his kingdom.

In the Saite [Sethroite] nome he found a city very favorably situated on the east of the Bubastite branch of the Nile, and *called Auaris (Avaris) after an ancient religious tradition. This place he rebuilt and fortified with massive walls, planting there a garrison of as many as 240,000 heavy-armed men to guard his frontier.* Here he would come in summertime, partly to serve out rations and pay his troops, partly to train them carefully in manoeuvres and so strike terror into foreign tribes.[10]

It is clear from Manetho's statement that Salities, the first of the Hyksos kings, made his residence at Memphis, although his successors must have moved their residence later to another city, such as Tell ed-Dab'a. He also refortified the border city with massive walls and left a great military garrison there, which became known as Avaris, where he would visit them once every summer. Thus Manetho's account makes it clear that, from the start, the Hyksos royal residence was not at Avaris, which was mainly a military garrison.

WHO WERE THE ANCIENT EGYPTIANS?

What is the origin of the early pre-Dynastic dwellers of the Nile Valley? Where did they come from?

G. Elliot Smith, the first professor of anatomy in the Cairo School of Medicine at Qasr el 'ani, at the start of the twentieth century, explained the difference between Egyptians and Arabs.

The Egyptian had developed the habit of shaving, whereas the nomadic Arab had not done so, and thus was represented . . . with a small beard reaching from the chin along the jaws in front of the ears. . . . The Proto-Egyptians presented a marked contrast to the Armenoid people of Western Asia, not only in their relatively scanty facial hair, but also in the glabrous character of their bodies generally. The body hair was very poorly developed in both sexes.[11]

While geographic evidence shows that the early Egyptians came from North and East Africa, Nubia and Arabia (through Sinai and the Red Sea), linguistic evidence also confirms this conclusion. The Egyptian language is related, not only to the Semitic tongues (Arabic, Hebrew, Aramaic, etc.), but also to the East African languages (Galla, Somali, etc.), and the Berber idioms of North Africa. Its connection with the latter groups, together known as the Hamitic family, is little studied as yet, but the relationship to the Semitic tongues can be fairly accurately defined. In general structure the similarity is very great; Egyptian shares the principal peculiarity of Semitic in that its word-stems consist of combinations of consonants, as a rule three in number, which are theoretically at least unchangeable. Grammatical inflexion and minor variations of meaning are contrived mainly by bringing the changes on the internal vowels, though affixed endings also are used for the same purpose; more important differences of meaning are created by reduplication, whole or partial. There are, moreover, many points of contact in the vocabulary.[12]

Modern science also confirms this conclusion. Luigi Luca Cavalli-Sforza, an Italian population geneticist and one of the more distinguished geneticists of the twentieth century, noted in his book *The History and Geography of Human Genes* that in the Nile Valley, Egypt has always been an African civilization though it straddles two regions: Africa and the Middle East. It is fairly clear that the cultural roots of ancient Egypt lie in Africa and not in Asia. Egypt was a subtropical desert environment, and its people had migrated from various ethnic groups over its history (and prehistory), thus it was something of a "melting pot," a mixture of many types of people with many skin tones, some certainly from the Sub-Saharan regions (in Africa) and others from more Mediterranean climes. It is impossible to categorize these people into the tidy "black" and "white" terms of today's racial distinctions. The Egyptians are better classified using evidence of their language and their material cultures, historical records, and their physical remains because so-called racial identification has been elusive. Skulls have been measured and compared, and DNA tests attempted in various forms, but conclusions are few. Skulls are more similar to those found in the Northern Sudan and less similar to those found in West Africa, Palestine, and Turkey. It seems that there has been some genetic continuity from pre-Dynastic time through the Middle Kingdom, *after which there was a considerable infiltration into the Nile Valley from outside populations*. That the Egyptians by and large were dark is certain, and many must have been what we today call "black." We can safely conclude that the ancient Egyptians were of various skin colors, few of which were light, judging by the climate.

12

WHICH RAMSES ARE WE LOOKING FOR?

As Exodus 1:11 states that the Israelites were forced to build Ramses as a store-city for the Pharaoh, scholars assumed that this was the same city built by Ramses II, known from Egyptian texts as Pi-Ramses, the House of Ramses, and regarded this king to be the Pharaoh of Oppression.

> That Rameses II was the Pharaoh of the captivity, and that Merenptah, his son and successor, was the Pharaoh of the Exodus, are now [end of nineteenth century] among the accepted presumptions of Egyptological science. The Bible and the monuments confirm each other upon these points, while both are corroborated by the results of recent geographical and philological research. The "treasure-cities Pithom and Raamses," which the Israelites built for Pharaoh with bricks of their own making, are the Pi-Tum and Pi-Rameses of the inscriptions, and both have recently been identified by M. Naville, in the course of his excavations conducted in 1883 and 1886 for the Egypt Exploration Fund.[1]

The Pharaoh of the Exodus, however, was not Ramses II, but his grandfather Ramses I, who established the Nineteenth Dynasty. It was this Ramses who had his residence in the fortified city of Zarw in northern Sinai, where he lived even before sitting on the throne. As the Bible states that the Israelites, when they were permitted to live in Egypt, were not allowed to enter the Nile Valley, but were allocated a border area known as Goshen, Ramses' residence at Zarw, the capital city of the border settlements in the Arabian nome, was certainly in the same location.

The Israelites were given a place named Goshen in the Bible, where they remained until the time of the Exodus and, although the word "Goshen" has no Hebrew meaning, Egyptologists have suggested it should be found in what the Greeks called the "Arabian nome" in the eastern desert. It is clear from the biblical narration that Goshen was somewhat apart from Egypt of the Nile: "Ye may dwell in the land of Goshen; for every shepherd is an abomination unto the Egyptians" (Genesis 46:34). The Children of Israel remained in this very area of Goshen from the time of their arrival until sometime later, when they were forced to build the store-city of Ramses, and left Goshen only when they left Egypt in their Exodus under Moses.

It was also at Zarw that Seti I, the second king of the Nineteenth Dynasty, was welcomed by the high priests and officials on his return from his first-year campaign against the Shasu alliance in Sinai and southern Palestine, as can be seen from the Karnak records. This indicates that the royal family at the start of the Nineteenth Dynasty must have had a residence in this area. The implication, as they had no means of knowing precisely when Seti I would return from his campaign, is that the high priests and officials who greeted him were residing in Zarw at the time of his arrival. As for Seti himself, both he and his father had been mayors of Zarw and commanders of its troops during the reign of Horemheb, and it is a logical deduction that he had had a residence there since that time.

The first mention we find of Zarw dates from the campaign by Ahmose I that resulted in the defeat of the Hyksos and the establishing of the Eighteenth Dynasty.

The war against the Hyksos may have lasted longer than is usually reckoned. . . . Yet the neglected colophon (written section) of the

Rhind Mathematical Papyrus tells of fighting in the eleventh year of an unnamed king. Since the main text of the papyrus is dated to the thirty-third year of Apophis, whom Kamose (brother and predecessor of Ahmosis I) opposed, this can only be . . . a successor. . . . On the twentieth of the first month (of Year 11) "the Southerner" invested the frontier fortress of Zarw, near modern Kantarah, and entered it a few days later.[2]

This account makes it clear that both Avaris and Zarw occupied the same site. From this point on, however, the name Avaris disappears completely from the texts and the next mention of this location is of Zarw alone, which occurs more than a century later, during the reign of Thutmose III and at the time of the first Asiatic campaign that followed the death of Queen Hatshepsut.

Year 22, month four in Peret, day 25 . . . Zarw, the first victorious expedition.

Later, during the time of Thutmose IV (1413–1405 BCE), his queen is known to have had an estate within Zarw indicating that, as well as being a fortress, Zarw became a settlement with a royal residence. Subsequently, Amenhotep III, the son of Thutmose IV, gave this royal residence to his wife, Queen Tiye, as a present. Later still, after the fall of the Amarna kings, who were descendants of Amenhotep III and Yuya, Horemheb, the king who succeeded them, used Zarw as a great prison where he gathered Akhenaten's followers, including the Israelites. There he appointed Pa-Ramses and his son Seti, as viziers and mayors of Zarw, as well as commanders of its fortress and troops. Thus Pa-Ramses, the new mayor of the city, was the one who forced the Israelites to build for him what the Book of Exodus describes as a "store-city" within his city of Zarw. Pa-Ramses followed Horemheb on the throne as Ramses I in 1335 BCE, establishing the Nineteenth Dynasty, and it was during his brief reign, lasting little more than a year, that Moses led the Israelites out of Egypt into Sinai.

At the time he came to the throne, Ramses I already had his residence at Zarw, being the city's mayor. Later, his son, Seti I, and grandson, Ramses II, established a new royal residence at the eastern delta known as Pi-Ramses, which became the capital of the Ramesside kings of the Nineteenth and Twentieth Dynasties, for about two centuries. The kings of the Twenty-first Dynasty moved to a new capital at Tanis, south of Lake Menzalah, and made use in its construction of many monuments and much stone from Pi-Ramses, which misled later scribes into the erroneous belief that Pi-Ramses and Tanis were identical locations.

However, instead of looking for the city of the Exodus at the land of Goshen and the border city of Zarw, Egyptologists went on looking for the city of Ramses II in the eastern delta, which they assumed to be at the same area as Avaris. In the 1960s Manfred Bietak, the Austrian archaeologist, excavated at Tell ed-Dab'a in the Sharkiya province in the eastern delta. He found a major Hyksos city that he, wrongly I believe, identified to be the Hyksos city of Avaris. Bietak gave an interim report in 1979 on his expedition's findings.

> To the north of Tell ed-Dab'a there is a natural lake basin while old survey maps, partly confirmed by the ground survey, show traces of a feeder-channel from the direction of the former Pelusiac branch of the Nile and a drain-channel flowing from the lake towards the larger Bahr el-Baqar drainage system. North and east of the lake remains were found of the Middle Kingdom (the Eleventh and Twelfth Dynasties ca. 1991–1785 BCE) and the Second Intermediate Period (ca. 1785–1575 BCE), at which time the Asiatics infiltrated the Eastern Delta and began the era of Hyksos rule there that lasted just over a century until they were vanquished in battle by Ahmosia, founder of the Eighteenth Dynasty (ca. 1575 BCE). Among other finds in this area was the lintel of a house belonging to Vizier Paser of Ramses II and, almost two miles to the east of Tell ed-Dab'a, an old well bearing the same king's name.
>
> In all, eleven strata were found. The remains at the very bottom belonged to the earliest settlement, starting some time before 1750 BCE, and the latest an early Ptolemaic settlement of a limited area,

dated to the third century BCE. The strata covering the Hyksos period (E3–1 and D3–2) are characterized by increasing density of occupation. The remains of two Canaanite temples were found, dating from ca. 1699 to 1660 BCE and 1660 to 1639 BCE respectively, and there was evidence that from about 1630 to 1610 BCE to 1610 to 1590 BCE the settlement began to develop its own Asiatic cultural line, *distinct from Syria and Palestine*. The site was largely abandoned after the Hyksos period, but occupied again toward the end of the Eighteenth Dynasty, the time of Horemheb. Remains of a temple were found, including a lintel of a sanctuary dedicated to "Seth, great of might" and bearing the name of Horemheb.[3]

Bietak summed up the expedition's conclusions in the following words.

To summarize briefly, apart from the later remains there is evidence, extending through a series of strata, of a huge town site of an Asiatic (Canaanite) community of the Syro-Palestinian Middle Bronze Age Culture IIA and B in the northeastern Nile Delta from the time of the Thirteenth Dynasty until the beginning of the Eighteenth Dynasty. Although several other sites of this culture have been discovered and identified since the beginning of our excavations, Tell ed-Dab'a is the largest and most impressive of all the sites and, by its fine stratigraphic series and abundant excavated material, the most representative.[4]

He went on to say that the temples of stratum E3–2 are Canaanite, and the size of the main sacred area excavated thus far shows that we have here, at the beginning of the Second Intermediate Period, the most important city-state of the Syro-Palestinian Middle Bronze Age culture in the eastern Nile Delta. It is not difficult to deduce, therefore, that the Asiatic community, after it had had time to establish itself in the eastern Nile Delta, must have been responsible for the Hyksos rule in Egypt. After a break in occupation we have evidence of a preplanned town of the Ramesside Period covering four to five square kilometers (some 250 acres).

In this final statement, Bietak was not commenting on the results of the excavations at Tell ed-Dab'a, but was referring to the remains at Qantir, another location just over a mile to the north. And what conclusion did he come to about the implications of the expedition's finding there?

> All the evidence taken together—the cultural and the stratigraphic—would fit well with the identification of the site on the one hand with the capital of the Hyksos, Avaris, and on the other with the delta residence of Ramses II, Pi-Ramses, as already maintained by M. Hamza, W. C. Hayes, L. Habachi, and John van Seters.[5]

Since then, there has been a general agreement among scholars on identifying Tell ed-Db'a/Qantir with Avaris/Pi-Ramses. Nevertheless, although Bietak's identification of Qantir as Pi-Ramses could be supported by archaeological evidence, his claim that Tell ed-Dab'a was the Hyksos city of Avaris lacks some important elements. While there is no doubt that Bietak has uncovered a major Hyksos city at Tell ed-Dab'a, this by no means proves that it was Avaris. All the sources we have about Hyksos Avaris confirm that, like Zarw, it was a fortified city. The Egyptian name of Avaris consists of two elements, *hwt-w'ret,* followed by a determinative, of a walled area. The first element, *hwt,* indicates a settlement surrounded by a high brick wall, the second element, *w'ret,* as Alan Gardiner has explained, signifies a "desert strip." So the very name of the city makes it clear that it was both fortified and at the desert border, just as Zarw was. This was precisely what one would expect in the case of invaders coming from the east in order both to protect themselves against the natives of the Nile Valley and remain close to their original home in Asia.

What persuaded scholars to regard Tell ed-Dab'a as Avaris is their wrong assumption that this city was the capital of the Hyksos rulers. However, if we look at the Manetho account of the Hyksos invasion, we find a clear distinction between the royal residence and the military fortress.

They (the Hyksos) appointed as king one of their number, whose name was Salities. *He had his seat at Memphis . . .* [while] in the Saite, he founded a city very favorably situated on the east of the Bubastite branch of the Nile, and called Avaris after an ancient religious tradition. *This place he rebuilt and fortified with massive walls, plantings, a garrison . . . to guard the frontier.* Here he would come in summertime, partly to train them carefully in maneuvers and to strike terror into foreign tribes.[6] (my italics)

It is obvious that Avaris was not the capital of the Hyksos from the very start, and although their king resided at Memphis during their early rule, they must have moved later to Tell ed-Dab'a. So while it is possible to agree with Bietak that he has uncovered the Hyksos capital at Tell ed-Dab'a, nevertheless, this could not be identified as the fortified city of Avaris.

On the other hand, while the biblical Ramses was related to the Hyksos capital of Avaris and in turn to the Eighteenth-Dynasty fortified city of Zarw as well as the Middle Kingdom's Ways of Horus, the city of Pi-Ramses was not. The Bible describes Ramses to be a "store-city"; that is why it was suggested that this refers to a fortress on Egypt's frontiers on or near the frontier, which would *not* be an appropriate description for the royal capital in the time of Ramses II. Exodus 13:17 indicates that the city of Ramses built by the Israelites was near "the way of the land of the Philistines," known from Egyptian sources as the "road of Horus," leading from Zarw to Gaza.

Because of this I have argued that the biblical city of Ramses must be found at the same location as the frontier fortified city of Zarw, to the east of modern Kantara, south of Port Said on the Suez Canal. Here the kings of the Twelfth Dynasty are known to have built a fortified city in the twentieth century BCE, which was mentioned in the autobiography of Sinuhi, a court official of the last days of Amenemhat I, the first king of the Twelfth Dynasty (1970 BCE). Sinuhi, who fled from Egypt to Palestine, mentions his passing the border fortress, which at that time bore the name "Ways of Horus." This same city was rebuilt and refortified by the Hyksos rulers who took control of Egypt during the mid-seventeenth century BCE. Under the Hyksos the frontier city became known as "Avaris." Later, when the kings of the Eighteenth Dynasty overthrew the Hyksos rulers, they, in turn, rebuilt this city with new fortifications, and gave it the new name of "Zarw," which became their main outpost on the Asiatic frontier, the point at which Egyptian armies began and ended their campaigns against Palestine and Syria.

When Muhammad Abdel Maksoud, the Egyptian archaeologist, started to supervise diggings at Tell Heboua, some two-and-a-half miles northeast of Kantara, in 1987, he thought that this location represented the fortress known from the war reliefs of Seti I at Karnak as "The Dwelling of the Lion," the first fortress guarding the road between Zarw and Gaza. After two seasons of excavation, Maksoud gave an account of his findings to members of the Fifth International Congress of Egyptologists in Cairo in November 1988, concluding his speech with the words: "It is possible now to identify the fortress of Tell Heboua with the 'Dwelling of the Lion' depicted in the reliefs of Seti I at Karnak."

Maksoud released some details of his findings at the end of the third season, and on reading them published by an Egyptian newspaper in April 1989 I realized that, without being aware of it, Maksoud had found the location of Avaria/Zarw, a view that was published by the *Sunday Times* of London a month later and has since become the subject of discussion by Egyptologists all over the world. What, in fact, had Maksoud discovered?

Fig. 12.1.
Muhammad Abdel
Maksoud. Photo
courtesy of Ahmed
Osman.

13

CLOSING IN ON THE LOST CITY OF RAMSES

On May 21, 1989, Roger Wilsher interviewed me for an article that was published by the London *Sunday Times*. A summary of the article appears below.

> The city from which Moses led the Israelites out of Egypt may have been discovered as a result of conversation overheard by chance by a young postgraduate student. Lost for 3,000 years beneath the mud and sands of the Nile Delta, the ancient city of Ramses I— who according to the Bible perished pursuing Moses across the Red Sea—is believed to have been unearthed after a century's quest and could strip away much of the legend surrounding the Exodus. The city's secrets will confirm some and contradict other aspects of the biblical epic of the persecution of the Jews. The site is at Kantarah Shark in Sinai, a region to the east of the Suez canal and thirty miles northeast of Qantir, the place most modern scholars had until now accepted as the lost city.

The *Sunday Times* article went on to talk about ruins that had been discovered by a team working for the Egyptian antiquities and led by Muhammad Abdel Maksoud, who did not, at the time, realize the significance of his discovery until November 1988, when he overheard a discussion that took place between me and another scholar, at the International Congress of Egyptologists held in Cairo. I was arguing with Manfred Bietak, the leader of the Austrian team excavating around Qantir. I doubted that Bietak's team had found enough evidence to be certain that they had uncovered the lost city of Ramses.

Since Bietak and his Austrian team began digging at Qantir in the Eastern Delta in the 1960s, he had been able to uncover a number of significant finds, including a royal palace built by the pharaoh Ramses II and surrounded by houses belonging to his nobles. In the nearby site of Khata'na, Bietak also found remains dating from the earlier Hyksos period—between the seventeenth and sixteenth centuries BCE—when the Hyksos rulers were controlling Egypt. This was an important discovery because contemporary papyri indicated that the city of Ramses II had been built on the foundations of the Hyksos capital, Avaris.

According to my research, the available sources indicated that Ramses was a fortified castle-like structure. Bietak had not found any evidence of this at Qantir and thus could not really establish his claim that he had found the lost city.

Muhammad Abdel Maksoud had been digging at Qntara East, in Northern Sina, for the Egyptian antiquity department, for the previous three years while preparing his Ph.D. from Lille University in France. After he heard the debate between Bietak and me, Maksoud claimed that he and his team "had found evidence of a massive walled fortification built on the foundations of an earlier Hykos city." Ali Hassa, director-general of antiquities in Egypt, agreed that Maksoud had found "an enormous fortress built over an ancient city" and a search would be led to find the palace of the kings.

The excavations at the site revealed the remains of a city of significant size, about 400 meters square, which had impressive fortifications suggesting a sizable military garrison. Maksoud and his team also uncovered some burial remains, remains of a temple and a palace, and large grain storehouses, which, according to the Bible, could suggest that they were built for pharaoh by forced Israelite labor. The city discovered by

Maksoud guarded the only route between Egypt and Canaan, known in Egyptian sources as "the Road of Horus." Maksoud also announced the discovery of the workers' quarter, including ovens that were used for baking clay for pots and building materials.

In my opinion this was an important discovery that would lend more credence to the story of Exodus and would give us the information needed to establish just what the Israelite route to Sinai was. It was likely that the remains of the people themselves would be found when the rest of the city was excavated, including houses and skeletons that had been well-preserved in the heat and sand.

In April of 1989, Bietak visited Maksoud's site, together with a number of other archaeologists. The Austrian archaeologist is reported to have said that, although he was impressed with what he saw, he still dismisses the idea that this location can represent the lost city of the Exodus. At the same time, some British Egyptologists agreed with Bietak's view, preferring to wait until the site had been fully excavated and examined and enough evidence emerged to convince them that this was the remains of Zarw, the fortified frontier city mentioned in the many texts of Egypt's Eighteenth and Nineteenth Egyptian Dynasties.

In my book, *Stranger in the Valley of the Kings,* I first suggested (in 1987) that Ramses was in the Kantarah region. Nowhere else has such evidence come to light, and the discovery confirms my belief that the three eastern Nile Delta cities mentioned in the Old Testament and other ancient Egyptian tracts were the same place.

14

DEBATE AT THE EGYPTIAN EMBASSY

Seventeen days after the publication of the *Sunday Times* article, Yuness el-Batrik, the Director of the Egyptian Cultural Centre in London, invited a panel of Egyptologists to discuss the subject on June 7, 1989. The panel included Professor Kenneth K. Kitchen of Liverpool University; Eric Uphill of University College, London; Jeffrey Spencer of the British Museum; Mr. Muhammad Abdel Maksoud of the Egyptian Antiquities Authority; and the author Ahmed Osman.

Maksoud presented his findings.

Having been working for three years at the site of Tell Heboua in the region of Kantarah in Northern Sinai, I found the largest fortified town in this region, known as the Eastern Gate of Egypt. This town was the largest and longest occupied *city* in this area, and the most ancient site in Northern Sinai.

Maksoud also reported that the city he had uncovered was constructed on top of at least two earlier cities. He stated that there were two different locations known as Tell Heboua, his site about 4 km (about 2.5 miles) northeast of Kantara, and another site near Kantara.

165

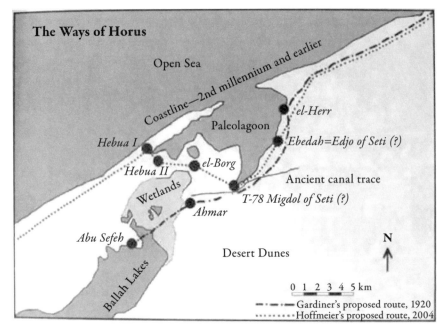

Fig. 14.1. Map of the excavated areas at Tell Heboua. From Revue
d'Egyptologie, *by Muhammad Abdel Maksoud and
Dominique Valbelle, January 2012.*

Maksoud regarded the city he uncovered at Tell Heboua to be "The
Dwelling of the Lion," the first important fortress along the military
road to Palestine, known as the Ways of Horus.

He also spoke of an important discovery at the site: a limestone
fragment in situ of Seti I, the second king of the Nineteenth Dynasty,
in the southern side of Tell Heboua, which he believed to be a temple
site; and two stelae of Nehesy, the first king of the Second Intermediate
Period who ruled from Avaris. Nehesy, who was the last ruler before
the Hyksos takeover, had the title "Beloved of Seth, Lord of Avaris."
Maksoud explained that he found the same evidence at Tell Heboua as
those found at Tell ed-Dab'a concerning the latter Second Intermediate
Period. We also have evidence that the town was occupied during the
Hyksos period. At least two cities were constructed one on top of the
other.

Although in the wake of the 1967 Six Day War, when the Sinai

Peninsula was occupied by Israeli forces, Israeli archaeologists were able to explore all areas in Sinai for fifteen years (1967–1982), they could not work at the site of Tell Heboua, as it became a military area due to its high position looking over the Suez Canal. However, following the Israeli withdrawal from Sinai as part of the peace agreement with Egypt, the Egyptian Antiquity Department began its investigation in the area of northern Sinai.

The site of Tell Heboua proved to be near the ancient Pelusiac branch of the Nile, between two lakes—north and south—on the western side of which are indications of an ancient canal at the start of what has now been established as the road of Horus. Remains of massive fortifying walls, more than thirteen feet wide, enclose a square area of some 190,000 square yards. Inside the walls are the remains of at least two ancient towns—one Hyksos, the other dating from the Eighteenth Dynasty—with houses, streets, storehouses, bread and clay ovens, and burials of two different kinds on two levels.

Maksoud, who conducted these excavations, found four identical stelae of Nehesy, the king of the weak Thirteenth Dynasty, two of which bear his cartouche. It was Nehesy (ca. 1715 BCE) who reestablished Seth as the main deity of the fourteenth nome. Seth had earlier been discredited as a result of development of the myth that had been responsible for the assassination of the good god Osiris. There was also a fragment of an architrave, belonging to a temple, with a cartouche of Seti I.

Although much of the site had not yet been excavated at the time, scarabs and other small items found there point to the existence of temples and palaces. Skeletal remains of children also make it clear that this was not simply a fortress but also a nonmilitary settlement during both the Hyksos and the Empire periods. In addition, Maksoud even found remains of an Asiatic community that had occupied the site before construction of the fortifying walls in the Hyksos period, indicating that the site had been occupied by a Semitic community during the Thirteenth Dynasty that preceded Hyksos rule in the eastern delta.

The most important evidence, however, was provided by the fortifications themselves. As well as being the only fortified city ever to have been found in the eastern delta, it has at least three different walls at

Fig. 14.2. The discussion panel at the Egyptian Embassy. From left Ahmed Osman (standing), Jeffrey Spencer, Kenneth Kitchen, Eric Uphill, and Muhammad Abdel Maksoud. Photo courtesy of Ahmed Osman.

three levels, confirming what is known from literary sources of Zarw, Avaris, and the Walls of Horus.

Maksoud concluded by saying that "the Tell Heboua remains proved to be the most important fortified town in this part of Egypt." However, as he had only two seasons of work, he regarded it as too early to identify the city whose remains he has uncovered.

Jeffrey Spencer, who followed, stated that "It has been mentioned that the city of Ramses would be expected to be a fortified city with a wall around it, and there are no walls and no evidence of walls and no evidence of any walls that have been recovered in the excavation in the region of Qantir." But he said that this was "not surprising," as the site of Qantir is now largely covered by cultivated land, and most of the mound of ruins—which marked the spot that the great city stood—have disappeared, leaving only ruins dot-

Fig. 14.3. Jeffrey Spencer.

ted around near Qantir, Khata'na, Ezbet Roshdi, and Tell ed-Dab'a to the south. However, Spencer did not explain how, if the thick walls have vanished, could ordinary houses, much less strongly built, have managed to survive in the very same layers and under the same conditions.

Spencer went on to talk about Qantir.

> The city itself had an extent of around 10 square kilometers, and if there were walls it is not surprising that the walls could not be detected because they were built of mud brick and would now be completely buried. . . . There may have been walls around the city of Qantir, which is generally believed to be Pi-Ramses, so it has not been detected. The different nature of the archaeology of the two sites makes it quite understandable why they have not been detected if they once existed. They may yet be located by some exploration in the future. Although there aren't fortified walls around Qantir, we do know that there was a lot of military activity at the site. So it was certainly a military base. This has been proved by recent excavations by Edgar Pusch, working for the Pelizaeus Museum Exploration at Qantir, where he has found large amount of military equipment; weapons, shields, parts of chariots.

He noted that at Tell Heboua the situation is different, as it was a desert site.

So clearly we are dealing with a location (at Qantir) which, in part, contained military bases, which would have served as the point of origin for the expeditions going up across Sinai, stopping by Tell Heboua on their way to do battle with the Asiatics. There is another difference between the two sites in that the Qantir/Tell ed-Dab'a reign was a city, I have mentioned its great size, great extent. Tell Heboua is a fort. It is not really a city, at least not in the Ramesside Period, not in the New Kingdom. The enclosure of the fort, 400 m. by 400 m., it is quite clearly just a defensive post, with the necessary buildings and stores to provision the expeditions, contained in it. And the layout of the buildings inside these walls shows the regular and design that we expect in military bases of that period. It is a military base.

However, the level underneath, the Intermediate Period level, that was a settlement quite clearly. It has characteristic housing of that period and rather more loosely arranged domestic buildings, and this quite clearly was an orderly settlement of the Hyksos. And it is not surprising that we find Hyksos living there. They controlled the whole region and their chief city, their capital, was at Avaris in Tell ed-Dab'a, or at least Professor Bietak believes it was at Tell ed-Dab'a, and I am quite happy to follow that view.

Again, whether there were walls around the Hyksos capital at Avaris/Tell ed-Dab'a, as is indicated by the inscription of Ahmose (son of Abana) of El Kab, this again set us from the same problem at Qantir the Ramses city, in that Tell ed-Dab'a is surrounded by cultivated land, and these walls may be difficult to detect, if indeed any traces of them remain.

I think my own personal preference would be to see the city of Pi-Ramses located in the region of Qantir centered on the location, which had formerly been at the end of the Hyksos capital at Avaris, now Tell ed-Dab'a. And to see Tell Heboua as a Ramesside fort built on the remains of a Hyksos settlement; one of the series of forts going up across northern Sinai, guarding the route for military expeditions, which originated at Pi-Ramses, and then travel up to the area of modern Kantarah, Tell Heboua, and then into Asia.

Eric Uphill thought that the location at Tell Heboua is very small to be identified as the residence of Ramses II, which should include many temples, statues, and stelae. Nevertheless, he suggested that Tell Heboua could represent the fortress of Zarw that appears in the Seti scenes at Karnak.

I would have thought that, given that it is safe, although it is very early days to judge, that this seems to be by far the biggest fortress in this chain of defenses. It would very well equate with one of those settlement scenes. This is a wide and wild suggestion I know, but one of them that comes to mind is Zarw, which I myself don't equate with Pi-Ramses, but I think is a major installation obviously something very big indeed. Maybe there is a canal in this area as shown in that scene (at Karnak). Zarw certainly was a major installation and Seti's scenes found at Tell Heboua appear to show that it looks like a gate or a window of appearances, and certainly stores as well as the granary.

Kenneth Kitchen agreed that the city discovered at the site of Tell Heboua belonged to the New Kingdom, which was established upon a town mount of an earlier period of the Second Intermediate Period and the Hyksos period, and may also be of an earlier period "with all these layers of occupation." However, he did not agree with Eric Uphill in his identification of the site as Zarw, and believed it would be "very wise to be cautious about saying the name it might have been in antiquity."

The point has been made as to one of these places has been built on top of each other. That is very clear in our good friend Muhammad Abdel Maksoud's site. He has got a lovely Second Intermediate Period site. A township of some kind at the top of which we get this fortress. And again, the fortress have had various sizes, 400 meters

Fig. 14.4. Professor Kenneth Kitchen. Courtesy of the Egyptian Exploration Society.

long. It is certainly a big and major fortress; there is no doubt of that. Whether it is actually Zarw or whether it is the Dwelling of the Lion, I don't know. None of us know.

Kitchen noted that "the Eighteenth Dynasty is neither represented at Qantir/Tell ed-Dab'a area, nor at Tell Heboua." This meant for him that

> none of these locations can be identified with Zarw. We need a site for the Second Intermediate, right to the Eighteenth Dynasty and then the Ramesside before we find the site of Zarw. This marvellous site at Tell Heboua is going to be one of the prime fortress sites. It could have a Palace where Pharaoh would stay overnight before his campaign in Palestine. It may well have a temple or two. Those sorts of possibilities our friend [Maksoud] might find.

In the meantime, as the walled city of Zarw found by Maksoud lies over a top mount, it seems likely that the walls of Avaris lie beneath it; and Ali Hassan, the head of the Egyptian Antiquity Organization, has admitted: "The remains found beneath the city are the first Hyksos remains to be found in Sinai and raise a new doubt regarding the position—now generally accepted as Tell ed-Dab'a—of the Hyksos capital in Egypt."

A sophisticated system of Egyptian forts, granaries, and wells was established at a day's march distance along the entire length of the road, which was called the Ways of Horus. These road stations enabled the imperial army to cross the Sinai Peninsula conveniently and efficiently when necessary. The annals of the great Egyptian conqueror Thutmose III tell us that he marched with his troops from the eastern delta to Gaza, a distance of about 250 kilometers, in ten days. A relief from the days of Ramses II's father Seti I (from around 1300 BCE) shows the forts and water reservoirs in the form of an early map that traces the route from the eastern delta to the southwestern border of Canaan. The remains of these forts were uncovered in the course of archaeological investigations in northern Sinai by Eliezer Oren of Ben-Gurion University, in the 1970s. Oren discovered that each of these road stations, closely corresponding to the sites designated on the ancient Egyptian relief, comprised three elements: a strong fort made of bricks in the typical Egyptian military architecture, storage installations for food provisions, and a water reservoir.[1]

Following this debate, however, Maksoud changed the subject of his Ph.D. at Lille University, from finding the "Dwelling of the Lion" at Tell Heboua, to finding "the city of Zarw."

15

EXODUS FICTION

As scholars insisted on searching for the Exodus evidence in the wrong location at the wrong historical time, they only achieved negative evidence. Neither Tell ed-Dab'a nor Qantir has produced any evidence to support the biblical account of the Israelites' arrival in Egypt in their Descent, or leaving it in their Exodus. At the same time, there has been extensive archaeological excavation in Egypt and Israel, as well as other lands of the Bible in the last century, with no positive evidence to announce. As a result, mainstream history and archaeology now consider the Exodus to have never happened, and the biblical story is an entirely fictional narrative put together between the eighth and the fifth centuries BCE, as modern archaeologists have concluded that the Bible stories can no longer be regarded as a source of history. Current Egyptologists and archaeologists deny that there was an Exodus, and claim that this story represented a confusion of the expulsion of the Hyksos from Egypt.

Although they still regard Judaism, as well as Christianity and Islam, as being the primary factual historical narrative of the origin of the Moses religion, Exodus is now accepted by scholars as having been compiled from stories dating possibly as far back as the thirteenth century BCE, with further polishing in later centuries BCE, as a theological and political manifesto to justify their history.

The theme of the Israelites' Exodus from Egypt and God's gift of the Promised Land to them is one of the most prominent in the Bible. Statements about these events are made in many biblical books in addition to the detailed treatment this theme receives in the books from Exodus through Judges. But in our search for the historical reality behind these biblical passages, we need focus only on those that are either earlier than Deuteronomy and the Deuteronomistic History. Since the Exodus and Conquest traditions in later works, like Chronicles or Ezra, could help us evaluate the antiquity and validity of the materials used by the Deuteronomistic historian(s). Neither are exilic and postexilic writings useful to us in determining whether the Genesis-Numbers accounts are *earlier* than the Deuteronomy, as most biblical scholars have believed, or *later* than the Deuteronomistic History, as a number studies now assert.[1]

Following a hopeful start in the nineteenth and early twentieth centuries, archaeologists have largely given up regarding the Bible as any use at all as a field guide. A large number of scholars now no longer agree that the biblical narrations of ancient Israel represent the historical fact. For many centuries, scholars have assumed that the Old Testament "events," such as the Descent into Egypt and the Exodus, actually occurred in the same manner it is reported in the Bible. However, this has begun to change. In the seventeenth century James Ussher (1581–1656), the Anglican archbishop of Armagh, in his treatise on chronology based on biblical dates, concluded that God created the world on Sunday, October 23, 4004 BCE.

Until the eighteenth century, the general belief was that the Earth was created about 4,000 to 5,000 years before the birth of Christ, and that the garden of Eden, the Flood, the Tower of Babel, and the stories of Abraham and the Exodus described actual events, constituting a genuine narrative history from Creation to the founding of Israel. A central pillar of the Bible's historical authority was the tradition that it had been composed by the principal actors or eyewitnesses to the events described; the first five books of the Old Testament were believed to have been written by Moses himself. However, Thomas Hobbes in his major work *Leviathan* denied Mosaic authorship of the Pentateuch. By the end of the nineteenth century the scholarly consensus was that the Pentateuch was the work of many authors written between about 1000 BCE and 500 BCE.

Later, in the second half of the nineteenth century, the school of biblical criticism developed in Germany. John Wellhausen, as the leading figure, challenged the historicity of the Old Testament narrations, claiming that it was written with a theological purpose. Then a new approach began in the United States early in the twentieth century with the emergence of the biblical archaeology movement under the influence of Albright, which sought to validate the historicity of the events narrated in the Bible through the ancient texts and material remains in the Near East. William Foxwell Albright (1891–1971) was an American archaeologist, biblical scholar, and philologist. From the early twentieth century, Albright was founder of the biblical archaeology movement and became the dean of biblical archaeologists until his death in 1971. He was also the Director of the American School of Oriental Research in Jerusalem before World War II and did important archaeological work in Palestine at the time. Albright regarded biblical archaeology as "the branch that sheds light upon the social and political structure, the religious concepts and practices, and other human activities and relationships that are found in the Bible." He advocated "biblical archaeology" in which the archaeologists' task is seen as being to illuminate, to understand, and in their greatest successes to "prove" the Bible, insisting that as a whole, the picture in Genesis is historical, and claiming that archaeology had proved the essential historicity of the Book of Exodus.

THE MINIMALISTS

After his death, however, Albright's methods and conclusions have been increasingly questioned. As more discoveries were made, and anticipated finds failed to materialize, it became apparent that archaeology did not, in fact, support the claims made by him and his followers. Albright's central theses have been overturned, partly by further advances in biblical criticism, but mostly by the continuing archaeological research of younger Americans and Israelis who had received encouragement from him. Since the 1990s two opposing scholarly schools appeared in regard to the interpretation of the Bible stories: the minimalist and the maximalist. While the minimalists deny the historicity of the biblical stories, the maximalists rely on the written evidence and regard the biblical accounts as historical. When a century of archaeological work in the Near East could not find evidence to support the biblical stories, some scholars dismissed the Bible as a reliable source of history. On the other hand, when archaeology's evidence contradicts the Bible, the maximalists argue that "the absence of evidence is not evidence."

Biblical minimalism—also known as The Copenhagen School—included people like Niels Peter Lemche, Thomas L. Thompson, Philip R. Davies, and Keith Whitelam. Relying on archaeological data, they regard the biblical stories of the Israelite Exodus from Egypt and their conquest of Canaan as nonhistorical, and argue that the Bible stories are largely mythical in nature.

One of the leaders of the minimalist movement, Thomas L. Thompson, Professor of Old Testament at the University of Copenhagen, explains his views in his book, *The Early History of the Israelite People.* He says that "the inevitable conclusion is that the Israelite exile in Egypt, the Exodus and Israelite conquest of the Promised Land never took place. All but few modern scholars have accepted the conclusion uncritically that the Hyksos were originally Palestinians."[2] He explained that in modern times scholars have thought the identity of the Hyksos to be Arabs, horse-breeders from Asia, Hittites, Indo-Iranians, or Hurrians.

The new consensus of Alt and the early Albright, which had been building prior to the Second World War, began to break up in the post-war years. Many scholars, following the lead of Albright's quest of extra-biblical evidence for Israel's origins, adopted the rapidly developing understanding of biblical archaeology as a means of confirming the historicity of the biblical traditions, especially of the patriarchs, Moses, and the exodus, the wilderness wanderings of the Pentateuch, and the conquest stories of the Book of Joshua. . . . With the publication of Bright's *History of Israel* in 1957 and Wright's

Biblical Archaeology in 1958, many scholars confidently spoke of the assured results of biblical archaeology for the history of early Israel: a patriarchal period well established in the extra-biblical history of the early second millennium, the authenticity of the Joseph and Moses traditions supported by our understanding of ancient Egypt.[3]

Donald B. Redford, the Canadian Egyptologist, suggested that the most evocative and consistent geographical details of the Exodus story come from the seventh century BCE, six centuries after the events of the Exodus were supposed to have taken place. Redford argued that many details in the Exodus narrative can be explained in this setting, which was also Egypt's last period of imperial power under the rulers of the Twenty-sixth Dynasty. He suggested that the Exodus narrative reached its final form during this time, in the second half of the seventh century BCE:

> There is perhaps no other scriptural tradition so central to the construction of Israel's history that Deuteronomy presents us with than the Exodus of the Hebrews from Egypt. It has become a prototype of salvation, a symbol of freedom, and the very core of a great world religion. Yet to the historian it remains the most elusive of all the salient events of Israelite history. The event is supposed to have taken place in Egypt; yet Egyptian sources know it not. On the morrow of the Exodus Israel numbered approximately 2.5 million (extrapolated from Numb. 1:46); yet the entire population of Egypt at the time was only 3 to 4.5 million! . . . yet at no point in the history of the country during the New Kingdom is there the slightest hint of the traumatic impact such an event would have had on economics or society . . . the Asiatic population in Egypt had lingered during the New Kingdom, and a part of it had been assigned construction tasks; but the "store-cities" of the Exodus story (1:11) are purely Israelite phenomenon, and the progressive assimilation of the Asiatic population during the New Kingdom is not reflected in the Exodus at all. Clearly something is wrong. Are we approaching the subject from the proper direction? The almost insurmountable diffi-

culties in interpreting the Exodus narrative as history have led some to dub it "mythology rather than . . . a detailed reporting of the historical facts and therefore impossible to locate geographically."[4]

Redford believes the Exodus story was an echo of the Hyksos descent and occupation of Egypt.

> The memory of this major event in the history of the Levant survived not only in Egyptian sources. It would be strange indeed if the West Semitic speaking population of Palestine, from whence the invaders had come in MB IIB [periods of the Bronze Age that started about 3,000 years BCE] had not also preserved in their folk memory this great moment of (for them) glory. And in fact it is the Exodus account that we are confronted with the "Canaanite" version of this event, featuring the great ancestral leader Jacob, the four-generation span, the memory of political primacy, the occupation of the eastern fringe of the Delta, and so on. It became part of the origin stories of all the Semitic enclaves of the area, and from there it even spread to the north and west where it became current among the non-Semites. . . . In sum, therefore, we may state that the memory of the Hyksos expulsion did indeed live on the folklore of the Canaanite population of the southern Levant. . . . It became not a conquest but a peaceful descent of a group with pastoral associations who rapidly arrived at a position of political control. Their departure came not as a result of ignominious defeat, but either voluntarily or as a flight from a feud, or yet again as salvation from bondage. Nor are we justified in construing as a difficulty the discrepancy between the bondage tradition of Exodus 1:11–14 and the historical reality of the Hyksos expulsion: the biblical writer has here incorporated another figment of legend for which, in fact, he had Egypt to thank.[5]

On the other hand, Israeli archaeologists, who themselves conducted excavation work in Palestine and Sinai, joined the minimalists, rejecting the historicity of the biblical account. Ze'ev Herzog provides the current consensus view on the historicity of the Exodus: "The Israelites never were in Egypt. They never came from abroad (outside Palestine). This whole chain is broken. It is not a historical one. It is a later legendary reconstruction, made in the seventh century [BCE] of a history that never happened."[6]

Two other Israeli academics and archaeologists, Israel Finkelstein and Neil Asher Silberman, have worked together to explain their views in a book, *The Bible Unearthed*. They start by raising some questions.

The heroic figure of Moses, confronting the tyrannical pharaoh, the ten plagues, and the massive Israelite Exodus from Egypt have endured over the centuries as the central, unforgettable images of biblical history. Through a divinely guided leader-not-a-father who represented the nation to God and God to the nation, the Israelites navigated the almost impossible course from hopeless slave status back to the very borders of their Promised Land. So important is this story of the Israelites' liberation from bondage that the biblical books of Exodus, Leviticus, Numbers, and Deuteronomy—a full four-fifths of the central scriptures of Israel—are devoted to the momentous events experienced by a single generation in slightly more than forty years. During these years occurred the miracles of the burning of the bush, the plagues, the parting of the Red Sea, the appearance of manna in the wilderness, and the revelation of God's Law on Sinai, all of which were the visible manifestations of God's rule over both nature and humanity. The God of Israel, previously known only by private revelations to the patriarchs, here reveals himself to the nation as a universal deity. But is it history?

Can archaeology help us pinpoint the era when a leader named Moses mobilized his people for the great act of liberation? Can we even determine if the Exodus—as described in the Bible—ever occurred? Two hundred years of intensive excavation have offered a detailed chronology of events, personalities, and places of pharaonic times. Even more than descriptions of the patriarchal stories, the Exodus narrative is filled with a wealth of detailed and specific geographical references. Can they provide a reliable historical background of the great epic of the Israelites' escape from Egypt and their reception of the Law on Sinai?[7]

They noted that Egyptian sources do confirm the arrival of Canaanite emigrants to Sinai and the delta.

One thing is certain. The basic situation described in the Exodus saga—the phenomenon of immigrants coming down to Egypt from Canaan and settling in the eastern border regions of the delta—is abundantly verified in the archaeological finds and historical texts. From the earliest recorded times throughout antiquity, Egypt beckoned as a place of shelter and security for the people of Canaan at times when drought, famine, or warfare made life unbearable or even difficult . . . the Nile once split into as many as seven branches and created a vastly large area of well-watered land. The easternmost branch extended into what is now the marshy, salty, arid zone of northwestern Sinai. And man-made canals flowing from it carried freshwater to the entire area, making what are now the arid, salty swamps of the Suez Canal area into green, fertile, densely inhabited land. Both the eastern branch of the Nile and the man-made canals have been identified in recent years in geographical and topographical studies in the Delta and the desert to its east.[8]

However, biblical chronology persuaded scholars to regard Ramses II as the Pharaoh of Oppression.

The expulsion of the Hyksos is generally dated, on the basis of Egyptian records and archaeological evidence of the destroyed cities in Canaan, to around 1570 BCE. . . . I Kings 6:1 tells us that the start of the construction of the Temple in the fourth year of Solomon's reign took place 480 years after the Exodus. . . . That is more than a hundred years after the date of the Egyptian expulsion of the Hyksos, around 1570 BCE. But there is an even more serious complication. The Bible speaks explicitly about the forced labor projects of the children of Israel and mentions, in particular, the construction of the city of Ramses (Exodus 1:11). In the fifteenth century BCE such a name is inconceivable. The first pharaoh named Ramses came to the throne only in 1320 BCE: more than a century after the traditional biblical date. As a result, many scholars have tended to dismiss the literal value of the biblical dating, suggesting that the figure 480 was little more than a symbolic length of time, representing the life spans of twelve generations, each lasting the traditional forty years. . . .

However, most scholars saw the specific biblical reference to the name of Ramses as a detail that preserved an authentic historical memory. In other words, they argued that the Exodus must have occurred in the thirteenth century BCE. And there were other specific details of the biblical Exodus story that pointed to the same era. First, Egyptian sources report that the city of Pi-Ramses ("The House of Ramses") was built in the delta in the days of the great Egyptian king Ramses II, who ruled 1279–1213 BCE. . . . Second, and perhaps most important, the earliest mention of Israel in extra-biblical text was found in Egypt in the stele describing the campaign of Pharaoh Merenptah—the son of Ramses II—in Canaan at the very end of the thirteenth century BCE. . . . No mention of the name "Israel" has been found in any of the inscriptions or documents connected with the Hyksos period. Nor is it mentioned in the later Egyptian inscriptions, or in an extensive fourteenth-century BCE cuneiform archive found at Tell el-Amarna in Egypt . . . the Israelites emerged only gradually as a distinct group in Canaan, beginning at the end of the thirteenth century BCE. There is no recognizable archaeological evidence of Israelite presence in Egypt immediately before that time.[9]

Choosing the wrong time for the Exodus led archaeologists to look at the wrong location.

Putting aside the possibility of divinely inspired miracles, one can hardly accept the idea of a flight of a large group of slaves from Egypt through the heavily guarded border fortifications into the desert and then into Canaan in the time of such a formidable Egyptian presence. Any group escaping Egypt against the will of the pharaoh would have easily been tracked down not only by an Egyptian army chasing it from the delta but also by the Egyptian soldiers in the forts in northern Sinai and in Canaan. Indeed, the biblical narrative would be to turn into desolate wastes of Sinai Peninsula. But the possibility of a large group of people wandering in the Sinai Peninsula is also contradicted by archaeology.

According to the biblical account, the children of Israel wandered in the desert and mountains of the Sinai Peninsula, moving around and camping in different places for a full forty years. Even if the number of fleeing Israelites (given in the text as six hundred thousand) is wildly exaggerated or can be interpreted as representing smaller units of people, the text describes the survival of a great number of people under the most challenging conditions. Some archaeological traces of their generation-long wandering in the Sinai should be apparent. However, except for the Egyptian forts along the northern coast, not a single campsite or sign of occupation from the time of Ramses II and his immediate predecessors and successors has ever been identified in Sinai.

Repeated archaeological surveys in all regions of the peninsula including the mountainous area around the traditional site of Mount Sinai near Saint Catherine's Monastery have yielded only negative evidence: not even a single shred, no structure, not a house, no trace of an ancient encampment. One may argue that a relatively small band of wandering Israelites cannot be expected to leave material remains behind. But modern archaeological techniques are quite capable of tracing even the very meager remains of hunter-gatherers and pastoral nomads all over the world. Indeed, the archaeological record from the Sinai Peninsula discloses evidence for pastoral activity in such eras as the third millennium BCE and the Hellenistic and Byzantine periods. There is simply no such evidence at the supposed time of the Exodus in the thirteenth century BCE.

The conclusion that the Exodus did not happen at the time and in the manner described in the Bible seems irrefutable when we examine

Fig. 15.1. The Monastery of St. Catherine at the foot of Mount Sinai.
Photo courtesy of Ahmed Osman.

the evidence at specific sites where the children of Israel were said to have camped for extended periods during their wandering in the desert (Numbers 33) and where some archaeological indication—if present—would almost certainly be found.[10]

> The historical vagueness of the Exodus story includes the fact that there is no mention *by name* of any specific Egyptian New Kingdom monarch. . . . The identification of Ramses II as the pharaoh of the Exodus came as the result of modern scholarly assumptions based on the identification of the place-name Pi-Ramses with Raamses (Exodus 1:11; 12:37). . . . Beyond a vague reference to the Israelites' fear of taking the coastal route (the Way of Horus), there is no mention of the Egyptian forts in northern Sinai or their strongholds in Canaan.[11]

16

UNCOVERING THE LOST CITY OF RAMSES

Following our London Egyptian embassy meeting in 1989, Muhammad Abdel Maksoud went back to Egypt to carry on his excavation work at Tell Heboua. During the following seasons he was able to find more interesting remains from the site. James Hoffmeier, Professor of Old Testament and Near Eastern Archaeology at Trinity International University, who excavated the site of Tell el-Borg, four kilometers away from Tell Hebua, explained how Maksoud was able to verify the location of Zarw.

The aftermath of the Camp David accords and the return of Sinai to Egyptian control witnessed a renaissance of archaeological exploration in North Sinai. Muhammad Abdel Maksoud in 1981 began to investigate various archaeological sites in North Sinai, many of which had been occupied by Israeli and the Egyptian armies and had suffered some damage as a result. Among his interests was determining the location of the key New Kingdom sites on the Ways of Horus and, in particular, the discovery of Sile/Zarw, Egypt's frontier town and strategic defensive fort. . . . Egyptologists have long wished to know the location of the frontier town of Zarw and its fort (*khtm*) because of its importance over many centuries.[1]

During the New Kingdom (ca. 1540–1100 BCE), a chain of Egyptian forts guarded the route running in northern Sinai between the Egyptian border city at Kantara and Gaza. On the other hand, the annals of Thutmose III, the great warrior who established the Egyptian empire in the Levant, contain the first reference of the "Fortress of Zarw," where it serves as the launching point of his campaign to the Levant. Later, Seti I battle reliefs at Karnak mention the Fortress of Zarw as the point at which he arrived returning from his war with the Shasu in Northern Sinai and southern Canaan. The Fortress of Zarw was also mentioned as the starting point of Ramses II's march against Kadesh with the Hittites. "Although it is not mentioned as a geographical term in Exodus, Zarw's location has been recognized as a possible reason why Exodus 13:17 explicitly states that the Israelites did not depart Egypt by the coastal highway, on the 'Way of the land of the Philistines.'"[2]

> Shortly after Egypt regained control of the Sinai, Muhammad Abdel Maksoud of the SCA began investigating a series of four closely related sites, called Hebua I–IV starting in 1981. He began to uncover a massive fort at Hebua I when excavations began there in 1985; these continue to the present . . . he initially thought that Hebua was the Dwelling of the Lion, the second fort on the military road . . . on the basis of the reliefs of Seti I at Karnak . . . But as the New Kingdom fort grew in size with further excavations, Abdel Maksoud began to change his mind, believing instead that Hebua was ancient Zarw, and that the fort at Hebua I was the Fortress (*khtm*) of Zarw. . . . Proof of this identification came with the discovery of a Ramesside-period votive statue found in the New Kingdom temple at Hebua I. Fortunately for me, I was in North Sinai on the very day it was uncovered in May 1999, and Abdel Maksoud and I were able to read the name of Zarw on the statue. Since the statue was found in the New Kingdom setting, it could not have been transported there at a later date, as after the New Kingdom the site appears to have been abandoned. . . . Consequently, we can be fairly certain that the ancient town site of Zarw was located at Hebua,

and the fortress mentioned in New Kingdom military contexts is the one uncovered at Hebua I.

What this discovery shows is that . . . Zarw was a formidable obstacle to the departing Israelites. Zarw had an enormous fort, the outside wall of which measures 800 by 400 meters and dates to the New Kingdom. But perhaps even more significant, it was located on the narrow strip of land, perhaps less than a kilometer across, with water on either side. Exiting Egypt by this route would have been a disaster for a force being pursued, and gaining entry to Egypt via this route by an enemy would have been a monumental challenge.[3]

Just over a kilometer southeast of Hebua I (which was the subject of the London debate) is the site of Hebua II, thought by Abe el-Maksoud to be connected to Hebua I (Zarw) because of its proximity. Between the two sites there was either a branch of the Nile (depending on the period) or a paleolagoon. While conducting an archaeological survey at Hebua II in 1992, a French team encountered New Kingdom materials on the surface, including part of an octagonal pillar with a partially preserved inscription that read: *sty [mr]n [pth] di 'nkh mi r'* (Seti [beloved] of [Ptah], granted life like Re). A brief season of excavations by the SCA there in 1999 revealed a New Kingdom complex of buildings with Nineteenth-Dynasty pottery and other remains, including a door lintel or cornice with the cartouches of Seti I on it. So, clearly, Hebua II is a New Kingdom site, and its location suggests to me that the direction of the route from Hebua I was toward the southeast. Because it is so close to the fort at Hebua I, Hebua II appears to be a part of Zarw complex rather than being the second fort in the Seti I map.[4]

So, while Hebua I, which was discovered first, represented the Fort of Zarw that was built above the Hyksos fortified city of Avaris, which itself had been built on top of an earlier Twelfth-Dynasty fortress, Hebua II, across a water canal with a bridge, represented the extension of the city of Zarw during the Eighteenth Dynasty. This picture agrees completely with Seti I's relief at Karnak, which shows a fortress on the Sinai side of the canal and a city on the delta side, both of which became known as Zarw.

Following new seasons of excavation, many new interesting remains were found, including a large temple built during the reign of Thutmose II and expanded during the reign of Ramses II. On April 22, 2009, Egyptian Minister of Culture, Farouk Hosni, announced that an archaeological mission working for Egypt's SCA had discovered the remains of a large New Kingdom temple in the area of Tell Hebua in northern Sinai. Excavators have found inscriptions in the temple dating to the time of Thutmose II, the fourth king of the Eighteenth Dynasty, through that of Ramses II. Hawass, Secretary General of the SCA, described the discovery as one of the most important ever made in Sinai. It is the largest temple known in the region, which was heavily fortified in ancient times because of its strategic location on Egypt's eastern border. The temple covers an area of some 80 meters by 70 meters. It is built of mud brick and surrounded by a four-meter-thick wall. It consists of four rectangular halls containing a total of thirty-four columns decorated with images of ancient Egyptian deities, including Horus, Hathor, Tefnut, Montu, and Renenutet. The temple also contains images of both Thutmose II and Ramses II.

Fig. 16.1. Farouk Hosni. Courtesy of BBC News, September 5, 2012.

Fig. 16.2. The god Horus offers Thutmose II the key of life, found at Tell Hebua (top). A line drawing of the artifact (bottom). From Revue d'Egyptologie, *by Muhammad Abdel Maksoud and Dominique Valbelle, January 2012.*

Zahi Hawass said that early studies of the temple indicate that it was an important center for Egypt's eastern border region. Its walls were brightly painted, and it housed three limestone purification basins along with a number of chapels. Muhammad Abdel Maksoud, the SCA director in charge of the region, said that to the east and west of the temple, the team found two groups of storehouses consisting of thirteen rooms each. These storehouses probably date to the reigns of kings Seti I, Ramses II, and Seti II. Inside, the team found thousands of inscriptions and seal impressions of Seti I, Ramses II, and Seti II. One particularly important example depicts Ramses I (ca. 1315–1314 BCE) before the god Set, the patron deity of the Hyksos capital of Avaris, now known as Tell El-Dab'a, in the eastern Nile Delta some fifty kilometers from Tell Hebua. He noted that, although four temples have been found in the area, only this one was newly discovered.

In January 2012, the French *Revue d'Egyptologie* published a report on these finds by Muhammad Abdel Maksoud, Director of Pharaonic Antiquities, and Dominique Valbelle, Paris University, Sorbonne.

Recent excavations in north Sinai (by the Supreme Council of Antiquities) conducted by Muhammad Abdel Maksoud since 2006, an important archaeological program in the site of Hebua II, situated about one kilometer to the southeast of Hebua I. These two sites correspond to the legend in the relief on the external wall, north of the Karnak hypostyle hall as the "Khetem (Fortress) of Zarw" . . . and the analysis of its components require taking into account not only the architectural features of buildings constituent, but also the institutional specificity of each of them. Geomagnetic recognition and several excavations have revealed the existence of a vast enclosure of 14 m thick, after dubbing, determining an area of 11 hectares within which two other ancient anterior we can put in evidence. . . . Space determined by the outer wall identified two sets of stores located respectively to the east and west and a small enclosure surrounding two buildings and their annexes. Various architectural elements and decorated monuments collected or recorded during the years 2008 and 2009 in the central buildings and their annexes, the stores east and west contribute to their interpretation. While the search continues and complements the elements already collected, [more] are likely to be discovered. The program of restoration and exhibition of these epigraphic testimonies original investigation [was] undertaken by the Supreme Council of Antiquities.[5]

The report mentions several successive levels were found in the central area, in two adjoining buildings. Their search is in progress and the respective dating of two main phases corresponds to the one at the beginning of the Eighteenth Dynasty, the other in the Ramesside period. Some decorated architectural elements from these constructions were found reused as forms of late furnished three graves in the northern perimeter of the building where only traces of the beginning of the

Fig. 16.3. Thutmose II sitting in front of offerings, found in a temple at Tell Hebua. From Revue d'Egyptologie, *by Muhammad Abdel Maksoud and Dominique Valbelle, January 2012.*

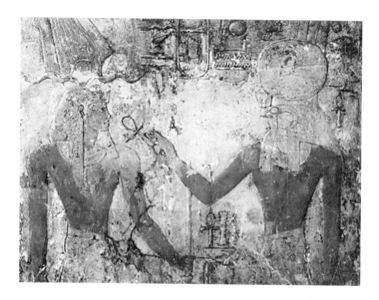

Fig. 16.4. Thutmose II faces Ra-Horacty in a temple discovered at Tell Hebua. Press release by Egypt's Minister of Culture, April 22, 2009.

Eighteenth Dynasty were identified. The report also mentions discovery of monuments decorated in low relief with the names of Hatshepsut and her husband Thutmose II.

Among the most important discoveries are the slabs of limestone and frames from a tripartite sanctuary, elevated and decorated internally during the reign of Thutmose II. Under that of Ramses II, the reverse of many of these tiles has received a relief decoration in the hollow. It was apparently during this period that some parts of the scenery of the Thutmoside period were damaged during the Amarna period, when any mention of Amun was cut off, but were later restored in sunk-relief.

The name of Ramses II was found under a grave dug in the bottom of the building north of the Eighteenth Dynasty remains, and Ramesside elements were found scattered in the central area. In addition, fragments of cornices and lintels enrolled were collected in the central area of the temple although we cannot determine their original source, as well as various fragments of large architectural elements, including entries on behalf of Ramses II, carved deeply in sunken relief.

Fig. 16.5. Ramses II offers the image of the goddess Maat to Horus, found at a temple at Tell Hebua. From Revue d'Egyptologie, *by Muhammad Abdel Maksoud and Dominique Valbelle, January 2012.*

Very significant for our argument, an arched stele of Ramses I, which measures 90.15 cm high, 58.5 cm wide, and comprises on both sides of the hanger, two legs, which witness of its installation. The king, turned to the left, offers two vases of ointment to the god Seth who faces him. While Ramses I wears a short wig loop equipped with an uraeus and ribbons floating over his shoulder, adorned with a gold necklace, the god Seth, who features the head of his sacred animal, is wearing a loincloth that goes up into the chest and with a belt on the abdomen closed with a knot of Isis. The accompanying text talks about "Seth, master of Avaris." Here as well, in the city of Ramses I at Hebua II, the remains of two stores were found, built at the start of the Nineteenth Dynasty, reminding us of the store-city of Ramses built by the Israelites. "The stele of Ramses I may as well commemorate the king's involvement in a local architectural program or simply his interest in site, as it may be a testimony of piety towards an ancestor."[6]

While Ramses I was adoring Seth of Avaris, names of the gods of Zarw were found at Hebua II, such as Amun, Montu Lord of Thebes, Hathor Mistress of Heaven, Horus Master of Zarw.

The excavation, since 2008, of the site of Hebua II, southeast of Hebua I, by a team from the SCA under the leadership of Muhammad Abdel Maksoud, led to the discovery of a rich epigraphic material either still in situ, or reused in late period tombs set in the ruins of the New Kingdom buildings. The report ends by pointing out that "the most important architectural elements are probably several large limestone slabs decorated on one side during the reign of Tuthmosis II [Thutmose] and Ramses II in the other. The inscriptions seem to designate Horus and Hathor as the principal landlords of the place."[7]

The remains at Tell Hebua I, which was built on top of at least two older fortified cities belonging to the Hyksos and the Middle Kingdom, have now been confirmed by archaeological evidence to be the location of the Fortress of Zarw. Moreover, excavation has revealed that during the time of the Eighteenth Dynasty a new extension of Zarw was built across the water canal as a residential settlement with houses and temples. It has also been confirmed Ramses I was worshipping the Hyksos Seth at Zarw, while new large stores were built in his city at the same time. I do believe that the name of Ramses in the Bible relates to this Ramses not to the grandson, as he had been a vizier and commander of the army, as well as mayor of Zarw before ascending the throne. Ramses I city of Zarw has been found, located at the start of the north Sinai route, the Ways of Horus, mentioned in the Book of Exodus as being in the vicinity of Ramses.

Thus the lost city of the Exodus has at last been found, confirming the historicity of this important biblical event.

NOTES

CHAPTER 3. EGYPT REMEMBERS

1. Josephus, *Against Apion*, 227.
2. Ibid., 258–59.
3. Ibid., 260–61.
4. Ibid., 281.
5. Ibid., 296–303.
6. Ibid., 281.
7. Redford, *Pharaonic King Lists, Annals and Day Books.*
8. Redford, *Egypt, Canaan, and Israel in Ancient Times,* 377.
9. Redford, *Pharaonic King Lists, Annals and Day Books.* 293.

CHAPTER 4. HYKSOS OR ISRAELITES

1. Josephus, *Contra Apionnem,* 205.
2. Ibid., 195.
3. Gardiner, *Egypt of the Pharaohs,* 156–57.
4. Josephus, *Against Apion,* 227.

5. FREUD'S DREAM

1. Freud, *Moses and Monotheism,* 15.
2. Ibid., 11.
3. Freud, Postscript to *The Question of Lay Analysis.*
4. Strachey, *The Origins of Religion,* 19.
5. Ibid.

6. Freud, *Totem and Taboo,* x, 142.

7. Rojzman, *Freud the Humanist,* 14.

8. Freud, *An Autobiographical Study,* 13–14.

9. Ibid.

10. Freud, *Totem and Taboo,* 1950, xi.

11. Ibid.

12. Jager, *Jewish Ideas Daily,* July 3, 2012.

13. Freud, *Moses and Monotheism,* 164–65.

14. Freud, E., and L. Freud, *Sigmund Freud: His Life in Pictures and Words,* 319.

15. Freud, *Moses and Monotheism,* 15–17.

16. Ibid., 20, 23.

17. Yerushalmi, *Freud's Moses,* 3–4.

CHAPTER 7. VELIKOVSKY'S MYTH

1. Velikovsky, *Stargazers and Gravediggers,* 27–28.

2. Callahan, "A New Mythology: Ancient Astronauts, Lost Civilizations, and the New Age Paradigm," 32–41.

3. Plait, *BAD Astronomy,* 181–82.

4. Ellenberger, "Falsifying Velikovsky," 204, 316, 686.

5. Velikovsky, *Ages of Chaos,* 26–29.

6. Ibid., 33.

7. Velikovsky, *Stargazers and Gravediggers,* 33.

8. Velikovsky, *Ages of Chaos,* 57–58.

9. "Vermin and Pests in Ancient Egypt," www.reshafim.org.il/ad/egypt/timelines/topics/pests.htm (accessed September 21, 2013).

10. BBC report, November 18, 2004.

CHAPTER 8. THE MIRACLE OF SANTORINI

1. Cameron, *Greek Mythology in the Roman World,* 124.

2. Hawass, *National Geographic News,* April 2007.

3. Ibid.

4. Vougioukalakis, *Associated Press,* April 3, 2007.

5. Humphreys, *Miracles of the Exodus,* 246.

CHAPTER 9. JOSEPH'S MUMMY IN THE CAIRO MUSEUM

1. Breasted, *Ancient Records of Egypt*, II, 345.
2. Peet, *Egypt and the Old Testament*.
3. Finkelstein and Silberman, *The Bible Unearthed*, 58–59.
4. Schulman, *Journal of the American Research Centre in Egypt*, Issue 2, 1963.
5. Cassuto, *A Commentary on the Book of Exodus*.

CHAPTER 10. MOSES AND AKHENATEN

1. Petri, *Researches in Sinai*.
2. Filer, *American Journal of Archaeology*, March 2002.
3. Hawass, *National Geographic*, August 2011.
4. Hawass, *Asharq Al-Awsat* (newspaper), October 29, 2009.
5. Zivie, *Archeology News Report*, December 5, 2009.
6. Giveon, *Les bédouins Shoshu des documents égyptiens*, 26.
7. Stavrakopoulou, *Discovery News*, March 18, 2011.
8. Gardiner in Bienkowski, *Early Edom and Moab*, 27.

CHAPTER 11. THE SEMITIC PHARAOH OF THE EXODUS

1. Pritchard, *Ancient Near Eastern Texts*, 253.
2. Bietak, *Avaris and Pi-Ramses*, 225.
3. Thompson, *The Mythic Past*, 141.
4. Finkelstein and Silberman, *The Bible Unearthed*, 55.
5. Thompson, *Early History of the Israelite People*, 195.
6. Midant-Reynes, *The Prehistory of Egypt*, 18.
7. Gnanadesikan, *The Writing Revolution*, 35.
8. Bard, *The Oxford History of Ancient Egypt*, 61.
9. Ibid., 61–62.
10. Manetho, *Ægyptiaca, frag.* 42, 1.75–92.2.
11. Smith, *The Ancient Egyptians*, 61–62.
12. Gardiner, *Egyptian Grammar*, 2.

CHAPTER 12. WHICH RAMSES ARE WE LOOKING FOR?

1. Blandford Edwards, *A Thousand Miles up the Nile*, 269–70.
2. Nims, *Thebes of the Pharaohs*, 199.
3. Bietak, *Avaris and Pi-Ramses*, 225–90.

4. Ibid., 271.

5. Ibid., 273.

6. Waddell, *Manetho,* 83.

CHAPTER 14. DEBATE AT THE EGYPTIAN EMBASSY

1. Finkelstein and Silberman, *The Bible Unearthed,* 60–61.

CHAPTER 15. EXODUS FICTION

1. Stiebing, *Out of the Desert,* 25–26.

2. Thompson, *The Mythic Past,* 141.

3. Thompson, *Early History of the Israelite People,* 77–78.

4. Redford, *Egypt, Canaan and Israel in Ancient Times,* 408–9.

5. Ibid., 412–13.

6. Herzog quoted in Sturgis, *It Ain't Necessarily So,* 74.

7. Finkelstein and Silberman, *The Bible Unearthed,* 48–49.

8. Ibid., 52–53.

9. Ibid., 56–57.

10. Ibid., 61–63.

11. Ibid., 65.

CHAPTER 16. UNCOVERING THE LOST CITY OF RAMSES

1. Hoffmeier, *Ancient Israel in Sinai,* 90.

2. Ibid., 91.

3. Ibid., 92–93.

4. Ibid., 97.

5. Maksoud and Valbelle, "Preliminary Report on the Decoration of the Epigraphic Archaeological Elements Discovered During the Campaigns 2008–2009 in the Central Area of the Fortress of Zarw," 1–2.

6. Ibid., 15.

7. Ibid.

BIBLIOGRAPHY

Bard, Kathryn A. *The Oxford History of Ancient Egypt.* Edited by Ian Shaw. Oxford, England: Oxford University Press, 2003.

Bienkowski, Piotre. *Early Edom and Moab: The Beginning of the Iron Age in Jordan.* Sheffield, England: J. R. Collins, 1992.

Bietak, Manfred. *Avaris and Pi-Ramses: Archaeological Exploration in the Eastern Nile Delta.* Oxford, England: Oxford University Press, 1979.

Blandford Edwards, Amelia Ann. *A Thousand Miles up the Nile.* London, England: George Routledge and Sons Limited, 1889.

Breasted, John Henry. *Ancient Records of Egypt,* II. Chicago: University of Chicago Press, 1906.

Callahan, Tim. "A New Mythology: Ancient Astronauts, Lost Civilizations, and the New Age Paradigm." *Skeptic,* 2008, 13 (4), 32–41.

Cameron, Alan. *Greek Mythology in the Roman World,* Oxford, England: Oxford University Press, 2004.

Cassuto, Umberto. *A Commentary on the Book of Exodus.* Translated by Israel Abraham. Jerusalem, Israel: Hebrew University, 1961.

Ellenberger, C. Leroy. "Falsifying Velikovsky." *Nature* 318, November 21, 1985.

Filer, Joyce M. *American Journal of Archaeology,* March [Anatomy of a Mummy, Archaeology Archive] a publication of the Archaeological Insitute of America, volume 55 number 2, March/April 2002.

Finkelstein, Israel, and Neil Asher Silberman. *The Bible Unearthed.* New York: The Free Press, 2001.

Freud, Ernst, and Lucie Freud. *Sigmund Freud: His Life in Pictures and Words.* Translated by Christine Trollope. New York: W. W. Norton & Co. Inc., 1978.

Freud, Sigmund. *An Autobiographical Study.* New York: W. W. Norton & Co., 1952.

———. *Moses and Monotheism.* Translated by Katherine Jones. London: Hogarth Press, 1939.

———. *The Origins of Religion,* vol. 13, *The Pelican Freud Library,* edited by James Strachey. London, England: Penguin Books, 1959.

———. *The Question of Lay Analysis.* New York: W. W. Norton and Co., 1978.

———. *Totem and Taboo.* New York: W. W. Norton and Co., 1950.

Gardiner, Alan. *Egyptian Grammar.* Oxford, England: The Clarendon Press, 1927.

———. *Egypt of the Pharaohs.* Oxford, England: The Clarendon Press, 1961.

———. In Piotre Beinkowski, *Early Edom and Moab: The Beginning of the Iron Age in Jordan.* Sheffield, England: J. R. Collins, 1992.

Giveon, Raphael. *Les bédouins Shoshu des documents égyptiens.* 1971.

Gnanadesikan, Amalia E. *The Writing Revolution.* Oxford, England: Wiley-Blackwell, 2009.

Hawass, Zahi. *Asharq Al-Awsat.* October 29, 2009.

———. *National Geographic,* August 2011.

Herzog, Ze'ev. In Matthew Sturgis, *It Ain't Necessarily So.* London, England: Charnwood Library, 2003.

Hoffmeier, James K. *Ancient Israel in Sinai.* Oxford, England: Oxford University Press, 2005.

Humphreys, Colin. *Miracles of the Exodus.* London: Continuum International Publishing Group, 2006.

Jager, Eliot. *Jewish Ideas Daily,* July 3, 2012.

Josephus, Titus Flavius. *Against Apion.* Cambridge: Harvard University Press, 1926.

———. *Contra Apionnem.* Translated by H. St. J. Thackeray. London and New York: Loeb Classical Library, 1926.

Maksoud, Muhammad Abdel, and Dominique Valbelle. "Preliminary Report on the Decoration of the Epigraphic Archaeological Elements Discovered During the Campaigns 2008–2009 in the Central Area of the Fortress of Zarw." *Revue d'Egyptologie,* January 2012.

Midant-Reynes, Beatrix. *The Prehistory of Egypt.* Translated by Ian Shaw. Oxford, England: Wiley-Blackwell, 2000.

Nims, Charles F. *Thebes of the Pharaohs*. New York: Stein and Day, 1965.

Peet, T. Eric. *Egypt and the Old Testament*. Liverpool: University Press of Liverpool, Ltd., 1924.

Petri, M. W. Flinders. *Researches in Sinai*. London: John Murray, 1906.

Plait, Phillip. *BAD Astronomy*. New York: John Wiley & Sons, 2002.

Pritchard, James B. *Ancient Near Eastern Texts*. Princeton, N.J.: Princeton University Press, 1969.

Redford, Donald B. *Egypt, Canaan, and Israel in Ancient Times*. Princeton, N.J.: Princeton University Press, 1992.

————. *Pharaonic King Lists, Annals and Day Books*. Mississauga, Canada: Benben Publications, 1986.

Rojzman, Charles. *Freud the Humanist*. London: Open Gate Press, 1999.

Rolnik, Eran J., and Haim Watzman. *Freud in Zion: Psychoanalysis and the Making of the Modern Jewish Identity*. Karnac History of Psychoanalysis Series. London, England: Karnac Books, 2012.

Schulman, Alan Richard. *Journal of the American Research Centre in Egypt*, Issue 2, 1963.

Smith, G. Elliot. *The Ancient Egyptians*. New York: Harper & Brothers, 1923.

Stavrakopoulou, Francesca. *Discovery News*. March 18, 2011.

Stiebing, Jr., William H. *Out of the Desert*. Amherst, N.Y.: Prometheus Books, 1989.

Strachey, William. *The Origins of Religion: Totem and Taboo, Moses and Monotheism and Other Work*. London: Penguin Books, 1990.

Sturgis, Matthew. *It Ain't Necessarily So*. London: Charnwood Library, 2003.

Thompson, Thomas L. *Early History of the Israelite People: From the Eritten and Archaeological Sources*. Leiden, Netherlands: Brill, 2003.

————. *The Mythic Past: Biblical Archaeology and the Myth of Israel*. London: Basic Books, 1999.

Velikovsky, Immanuel. *Ages of Chaos*. London: Paradigma, 2009.

————. *Stargazers and Gravediggers*. New York: William Morrow & Co., 1983.

Waddell, W. G. *Manetho*. Cambridge, Mass.: Harvard University Press, 1940.

Yerushalmi, Yosef Hayim. *Freud's Moses*. New Haven, Conn.: Yale University Press, 1991.

Zivie, Alain-Pierre. *Archeology News Report*, December 5, 2009.

INDEX

Page numbers in *italics* refer to illustrations

BOOKS OF RELATED INTEREST

Moses and Akhenaten

The Secret History of Egypt at the Time of the Exodus

by Ahmed Osman

The Hebrew Pharaohs of Egypt

The Secret Lineage of the Patriarch Joseph

by Ahmed Osman

Jesus in the House of the Pharaohs

The Essene Revelations on the Historical Jesus

by Ahmed Osman

Christianity: An Ancient Egyptian Religion

by Ahmed Osman

Breaking the Mirror of Heaven

The Conspiracy to Suppress the Voice of Ancient Egypt

by Robert Bauval and Ahmed Osman

Black Genesis

The Prehistoric Origins of Ancient Egypt

by Robert Bauval and Thomas Brophy, Ph.D.

The Temple of Solomon

From Ancient Israel to Secret Societies

by James Wasserman

Judas of Nazareth

How the Greatest Teacher of First-Century Israel Was Replaced by a Literary Creation

by Daniel T. Unterbrink

INNER TRADITIONS • BEAR & COMPANY
P.O. Box 388
Rochester, VT 05767
1-800-246-8648
www.InnerTraditions.com

Or contact your local bookseller